CAT BIZ

Amanda O'Neill

CAT BIZ

BARRON'S

First published in the United States and Canada in 2007 by Barron's Educational Series, Inc.

Originally published in 2006 by Interpet Publishing.

All inquiries should be addressed to:
Barron's Educational Series, Inc.
250 Wireless Boulevard
Hauppauge, NY 11788
www.barronseduc.com

Library of Congress Control Number 2005933432

ISBN-10: 0-7641-3467-1
ISBN-13: 978-0-7641-3467-8

Printed in China
9 8 7 6 5 4 3 2

Disclaimer

The information and recommendations in this book are given without any guarantees on behalf of the author and publisher, who disclaim any liability with the use of this material.

The Author

Amanda O'Neill was born in Sussex, England, in 1951 and educated at the University of Exeter, where she studied medieval literature. She has written books on subjects ranging from needlework to mythology, but her abiding interest has always been the world of cats and dogs. She has written more than 20 books on this theme, including *Cats and Dogs*, *The Mitchell Beazley Pocket Guide To Cats*, *Cats*, *The Best Ever Book of Dogs*, *What Dog?,* and the companion title to this volume, *Dogbiz*. She is a regular contributor to a number of national pet magazines in the U.K.

CONTENTS

continued...

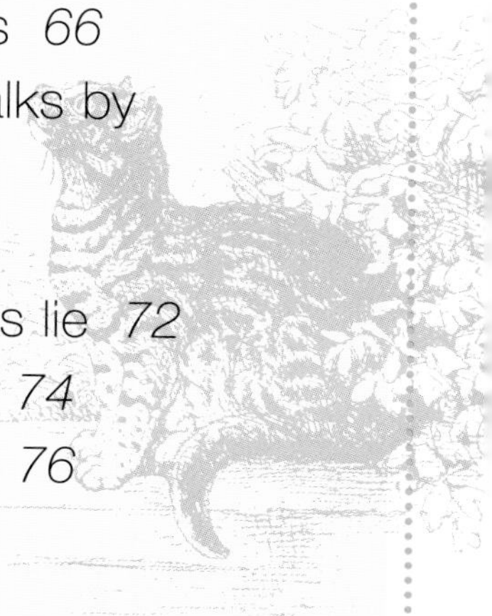

Section Two
The things cats do 78

Section Three
How we see cats 110

LOOKING AT

CATS

HOW THE CAT BEGAN

Legendary beginnings

Hebrew legend says that cats were created on Noah's Ark to tackle a plague of mice. When Noah prayed for help, the lion gave a giant sneeze—and the first cat burst out of his nostrils, ready to save the day. However, medieval folklore ascribes the first cat to the devil's unsuccessful attempt to make a man. His creation was such a pathetic specimen that St. Peter took pity on it, made it a fur coat, and invented the cat.

Made in Egypt

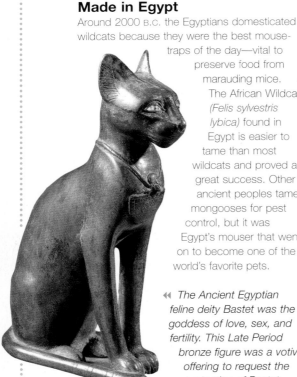

Around 2000 B.C. the Egyptians domesticated wildcats because they were the best mouse-traps of the day—vital to preserve food from marauding mice. The African Wildcat *(Felis sylvestris lybica)* found in Egypt is easier to tame than most wildcats and proved a great success. Other ancient peoples tamed mongooses for pest control, but it was Egypt's mouser that went on to become one of the world's favorite pets.

The Ancient Egyptian feline deity Bastet was the goddess of love, sex, and fertility. This Late Period bronze figure was a votive offering to request the protection of Bastet.

These mummified remains of a cat were found at Abydos in Egypt. They date from the first century B.C.

The mummy business

Mummified cats were buried in special cemeteries, some with carved stone sarcophagi and even mummified mice for an afterlife snack. But this honor had a sting in the tail: cat mummies were big business, and temple cats were bred and killed for the purpose. So many cat mummies were made that 19th-century archaeologists grew blasé: in 1889 a consignment of 19.5 tons of cat mummies shipped to England was sold as fertilizer.

The cat deified

Egypt's gods manifested in animal form—bulls, jackals, falcons, serpents. A latecomer to the divine menagerie, the cat soon found a niche as an aspect of the sun god Ra. Later, however, it became the sacred animal of the goddess Bastet, whose cult became immensely popular from the seventh century B.C., giving the cat a religious status unparalleled in history.

Ultimate cat lovers

Life in Ancient Egypt really pandered to a cat's sense of importance. Wall paintings and thousands of statuettes bear witness to the respect in which cats were held. Household pets were mourned with the same rituals as humans, and killing a cat incurred the death penalty—one Roman delegate who killed one accidentally was lynched by an angry mob. Understandably, an inscription of around 332 B.C. advises, "Do not laugh at a cat."

This Ancient Egyptian cat deity, a supporter of the sun god Ra, is seen slaying the serpent of darkness, Apep, so enabling the sun to rise.

Oldest cat name

The first recorded cat name in history in Nedjem ("sweet" or "pleasant"), inscribed in a tomb at Thebes dated to the reign of Pharaoh Thutmose III (1479–1425 B.C.). Egyptian carvings of dogs often include their names, but this is the only known example of a named cat.

Modern replica

Today admirers of the cats of Ancient Egypt can buy replica statuettes, but for some breeders this was not enough. In the 1950s European breeders developed a new breed, the Egyptian Mau, designed to resemble the elegant spotted cats of Egyptian wall paintings. Occurring in shades of black, smoke, pewter, bronze, and silver, the Egyptian Mau is a beautiful replica of its ancient ancestors.

A smoke-colored Egyptian Mau. This has the distinction of being the only naturally spotted breed of cat. It is thought to be descended from the African Wildcat.

WORLD TAKEOVER

Roman raiders

Egyptian laws strictly forbade the export of cats, but the Roman invasion of Egypt in 30 B.C. changed matters. Egypt became a Roman province, and her cats found their way into the hands of Roman troops and Phoenician traders. By A.D. 500 cats were distributed throughout the Mediterranean region, while back home in Egypt Bastet's cult was replaced by Christianity and her cats reverted from gods back to mere mousers.

The British cat

Britain's native wildcat has rarely been tamed successfully, so there was a niche awaiting the descendants of the gentler African Wildcat. The domestic cat was probably introduced by traders before the Roman invasion of A.D. 43 and quickly made itself at home. Roman settlers in Britain certainly shared their villas with cats, who left "feline graffiti" in the form of pawprints imprinted on tiles.

A Roman mosaic from Pompeii (first century B.C.) depicts this spotted tabby, caught in the act of stealing a partridge from the larder shelf.

Silk guardians

The Romans also introduced cats to China, but here they seem to have disappeared without a trace until they were reintroduced around A.D. 1000 via the Silk Route. Set to work as pest control officers, protecting precious silkworm cocoons from rats and mice, they were so highly valued that for centuries Chinese cats were kept on dainty chains and not allowed to run loose.

An early eighth-century Chinese cat is depicted in this pottery figurine of a horse and rider, from the tomb of a Tang Dynasty princess.

Japanese aristo-cats

Cats reached Japan around 600 A.D. Initially workers (Buddhist monasteries were required to keep cats to protect holy manuscripts from mice), they became aristocratic pets under tenth-century Emperor Ichijo, a true cat addict. Ichijo's edict that cats should not be set to work was not a success—pottery cats proved far less successful as mouse deterrents than the real thing—but for centuries they held noble status.

American pioneers

When the Pilgrim Fathers reached the U.S. on the *Mayflower* in 1620, they brought cats with them (including a "three-colored" female that produced a litter shortly after landing). Working cats were highly valued by the settlers and their descendants—indeed, during the California gold rush of 1849 miners paid $50 each for "guaranteed ratters"—and eventually they gave rise to the modern American Shorthair.

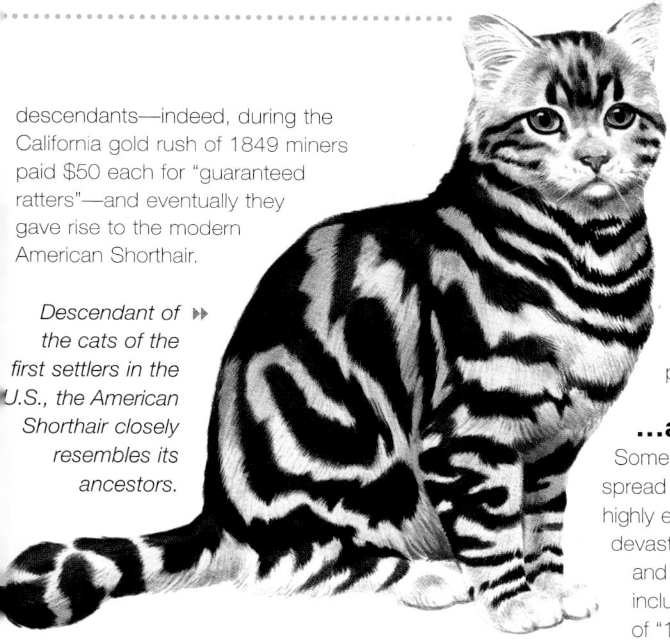

Descendant of the cats of the first settlers in the U.S., the American Shorthair closely resembles its ancestors.

Cats down under

When the First Fleet sailed from England to Australia in 1787, they too took cats with them. However, geneticists believe the cat beat European settlers to Australia by some three centuries, brought by Indonesian traders. By the mid-19th century feral cats were established in the wild, and today are the subject of heated debate as to whether they are a serious threat to native wildlife or scapegoats for humans' mismanagement of the environment.

Worldwide popularity

From Egypt, cats have been introduced across the world, missing out only some isolated islands in the southwest Pacific. There are an estimated 9 million pet cats in the U.K., 65 million in the U.S., and 2.6 million in Australia—plus uncountable strays, free-ranging farm cats, and ferals. Today they are taking over from the dog as the most popular pet of all.

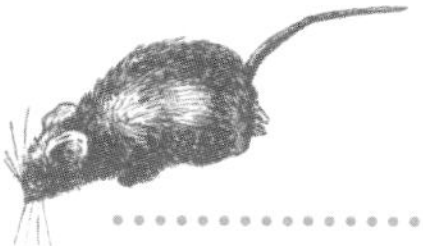

...and unpopularity

Some would argue that the cat's spread has been too successful. As a highly efficient predator, it has often had devastating effects on native wildlife, and the World Conservation Union includes the domestic cat on its list of "100 of the World's Worst Invasive Alien Species." Indeed, in 1894 a New Zealand lighthouse keeper's cat entered history by wiping out a whole species (the Stephens Island Wren) single-handedly.

Wherever there are food stores, mousers are in demand to tackle mice and rats.

BREED FACT FILE

What is a breed?

Technically, a breed is a strain that breeds true for certain distinguishing characteristics, and is recognized as a distinct breed by the cat fancy—but not all countries agree on which strains are recognized as breeds. Despite the popularity of purebred cats, they remain a minority. Only an estimated 3 percent of the world's cats belong to a breed—the rest are nonpedigrees or "moggies."

What is a variant?

A variant is a cat that, although purebred, has a color or coat type that does not match the breed standard. Variants are usually throwbacks to some forgotten ancestor. Sometimes a variant may develop into a breed in its own right. For example, some registries accept the long-haired Abyssinian variant as a Somali.

What are the most popular breeds?

TOP TEN *(based on registration statistics)*

	U.S.	U.K.
1	Persian	British Shorthair
2	Maine Coon	Siamese
3	Exotic Shorthair	Persian
4	Siamese	Bengal
5	Abyssinian	Burmese
6	Ragdoll	Birman
7	Birman	Maine Coon
8	Oriental Shorthair	Ragdoll
9	American Shorthair	Exotic Shorthair
10	Tonkinese	Oriental Shorthair

Where do new breeds come from?

"Recipes" for new breeds include crosses of existing breeds (e.g., Burmilla-Burmese x Chinchilla), hybridization (e.g., Chausie-domestic cat x jungle cat), and mutations (e.g., Rexes). The Ocicat was an accidental by-product of an attempt to produce ticked colorpoints, in contrast to the Toyger (still in development), a "designer breed" deliberately produced to imitate the tiger's "candle-flame" stripes.

The Burmilla (right) is a British creation dating back to 1964, and the Ocicat (left) is American, first appearing in 1981. Both breeds now come in various colors.

Said to be the oldest British cat variety, the British Shorthair is a sturdy, compact breed.

How many breeds are there?

Worldwide, more than a hundred breeds are recognized, but not all countries acknowledge all breeds. Europe's Fédération Internationale Feline (FIFe) lists 37 breeds, America's Cat Fanciers' Association (CFA) lists 37 breeds plus four in development, and Britain's Governing Council of the Cat Fancy (GCCF) lists 54 breeds—but there are also hundreds of varieties within the recognized breeds.

Why might some breeds be banned?

Some European countries ban breeds with potential health problems, such as Manx (spinal defects), Sphynx (hairlessness), Scottish Fold (skeletal disorders), Munchkin (dwarfism), and Blue-Eyed Whites (deafness). Other countries accept these breeds on the basis that caring breeders strive to produce healthy cats.

Have any breeds become extinct?

Yes, breeds sometimes disappear. Older breeds now lost include the Mexican Hairless and the Sumxu or Chinese Lop, a drop-eared cat from the Peking region. Some experimental breeds such as the Kinkalow (American Curl x Munchkin, with curled ears and short legs) never make the grade, perhaps lacking appeal or simply resembling existing breeds too closely.

What is the oldest breed?

Breeds known to have been in existence before the 19th century introduced the idea of pedigree cats include the Norwegian Forest Cat, Persian, Russian Blue, Turkish Van, Angora, Japanese Bobtail, Chartreux, Siamese, Korat, and Burmese. Some consider the Egyptian Mau the oldest breed, believing it to be descended directly from the Pharaohs' cats; but probably the humble non-pedigree cat has the best claim.

Van cats date back to the Middle Ages, but they were not known in the West until 1955.

A BREED TOO FAR?

Dachshund cats

Probably the oddest breed is the Munchkin, a cat with short legs like a dachshund's. The short-legged mutation has cropped up from time to time in different parts of the world, but it was Blackberry, a black stray discovered in Louisiana in 1983, who founded the new breed. Also known as the Louisiana Creole Cat, Wiener Cat, and Feline Ferret, the Munchkin was formally named after the little people in *The Wizard of Oz.*

A gene similar to that found in Dachshunds and Basset Hounds is responsible for the Munchkin's dramatically shortened legs.

Designer cats

Two Munchkin cousins developed in the late 1990s are the Minskin and the Skookum. Minskins (Munchkin cross Sphynx), described as hobbitlike, are short-legged cats with a "fur-point" coat, sparse on the body and denser on the mask, ears, legs, and tail. Skookums (Munchkin cross LaPerm) combine short legs with a rex coat and are described as feline Shirley Temples—short, sweet, and curly haired.

Peke-faced cats

In the 1930s a mutation appeared among American Red Persians with a flat face like a Pekingese. The Peke-faced Persian became a brief craze in the U.S. for its novelty value, but was rejected by other countries because of health problems. The foreshortened face caused snuffling and watery eyes, and most cat lovers preferred healthier pets.

Floppy cats

Ragdolls are the most laid-back of cats. They go limp and floppy when handled, and were initially said to be incapable of feeling pain. Indeed, there were ludicrous claims that the founder dam's genes were somehow changed by a car accident, or that skunk or raccoon genes were introduced. Initially associations refused to accept the breed, but they are now popular as handsome, sweet-natured, and perfectly normal cats.

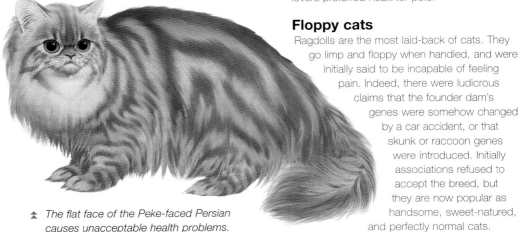

The flat face of the Peke-faced Persian causes unacceptable health problems.

...and flappy cats

A 1980s project based in the southern United States to develop the ideal barn cat led to the development of a new breed, the Keuda, which has a uniquely loose skin falling into conspicuous flaps on the belly and under the elbows. It is said that this allows the cats to extend their legs farther when running or defending themselves. The name is an acronym from the project's title, "Kitten Evaluation Under Direct Assessment."

Twisty cats

Twisty cats, or "kangaroo cats," are born with defective, abnormally short forelegs, so that they have to hop around on their hind legs like kangaroos. A short-lived attempt to found a new breed that would genetically pass on this deformity to their offspring met with violent objections from cat lovers. With patience and loving care, such handicapped cats can lead a reasonably happy life, but to breed the animals on purpose was rightly seen as unjustifiable.

This Chocolate Point Bicolor adult and Lilac Point Bicolor kitten demonstrate two of the attractive Ragdoll color schemes.

Nonallergenic cats

Quite a lot of people are allergic to cats. Some hoped that hairless cats like the Sphynx would solve their problems, but it is now known that the irritant is not cat fur but a protein present in cats' dander and saliva. Biotechnicians are striving to produce genetically modified, nonallergenic cats—not a new breed but a patented laboratory strain—that they hope to market to allergic cat lovers.

LABELING CATS

Purebred, or not?

Pedigree cats have a known and documented family tree. **Purebred** cats have ancestors all of the same breed. Generally the two labels mean the same thing—but not always. Some breed standards permit crossbreeding with certain other breeds to improve desired characteristics, so a pedigree cat may not be technically purebred. Equally, not all purebred cats have pedigrees: their origins may be unrecorded.

This feral cat from Crete has the almond eye shape associated with Eastern breeds.

Eye shape

Most wildcats have slanted, oval eyes, but selective breeding has developed varying eye shapes in modern cats. Some (typically Western breeds such as British Shorthairs) have very **round** eyes; others (typically Eastern breeds such as Birmans) have **almond-shaped** eyes. Some breed standards specify very exact shapes, such as the Russian Blue, whose eyes must be **almost round** but just oval enough to show an Oriental slant.

MARKINGS	
Self or Solid	One solid color with no markings
Mask	Dark color covering face
Hood	Colored mask extending all the way up to the base of the ears
Mitts or Gloves	White feet, as seen in, e.g., Birman, Ragdoll
Laces	White markings up the back of the hind leg, beyond the gloves, in Birmans
Blaze	Stripe or splash or white on forehead or nose
Bracelets	Dark stripes on the legs of a tabby
Penciling	Delicate markings like pencil lines on the face of a tabby
Ticking	Each hair banded in two or three colors, as seen in Abyssinians
Tipping	The tips of each hair a different color from the shaft, as seen in Chinchillas
Points	The darker areas of a colorpoint, i.e., face, ears, legs, and tail
Van pattern	Mainly white with color restricted to head and tail, e.g., Turkish Van

CAT TERMINOLOGY

	TERM	MEANING	BREED EXAMPLE
Body shape	Cobby	Stocky, compact, heavy boned, short bodied, and short legged	Persian, Exotic Shorthair, Manx
	Foreign	Slender, fine-boned, elegant, long limbed	Siamese
	Semi-Cobby	Medium shape, more cobby than foreign	British Shorthair
	Semi-Foreign	Medium shape, more foreign than cobby	Burmese, Abyssinian
Head shape	Round	Short round head, short ears, short nose, flattish face	Persian
	Wedge	Long, narrow head, large ears, long nose	Siamese
	Modified wedge	Longish head, less extreme than that of Siamese	Tonkinese
Colors	Usual	Original color of a breed, distinguished from color varieties developed later	Abyssinian (golden brown)
	Variety	Color form within a breed	Most breeds
Show type	Traditional	"Old-fashioned": bred to resemble older type less extreme than modern version	Siamese, Abyssinian
	Classic	Contemporary show type, usually differing somewhat from early specimens	Siamese
	Ultra	Bred for exaggerated show points, e.g., where the breed standard requires a "flat" face, breeding even flatter faces	Persian

CAT STATS—SIZE SURPRISE

How big is a cat?

The average cat weighs somewhere in the range of 7–12 lb. (2–3 kg), but there are extremes. Large breeds like the Ragdoll and Maine Coon may weigh 20 lb. (9 kg) or more, whereas small breeds like the Singapura may weigh as little as 4 lb. (1.8 kg) and Teacup Persians (a breed still in the experimental stage) a mere 2 lb. (0.9 kg).

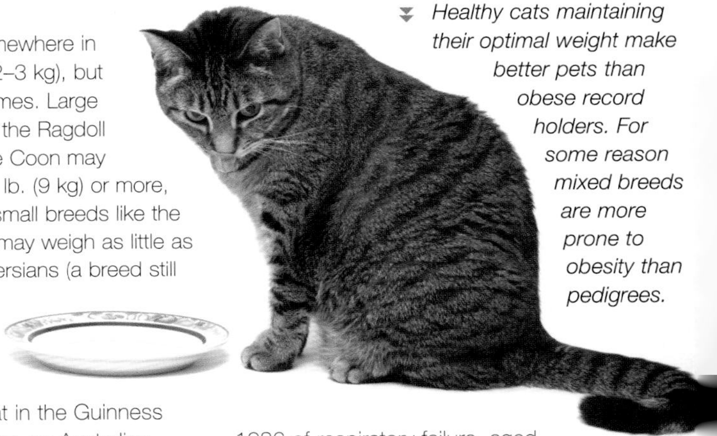

Healthy cats maintaining their optimal weight make better pets than obese record holders. For some reason mixed breeds are more prone to obesity than pedigrees.

Official fat cat

The last official Heaviest Cat in the Guinness Book of Records was Himmy, an Australian tabby weighing 47 lb. (21 kg) and with a 15-in. (38-cm) neck and a 33-in. (84-cm) waist. Himmy had to be pushed around in a wheelbarrow, and died in 1986 of respiratory failure, aged ten. Guinness no longer features this category in its book of records to discourage competitive owners from overfeeding their pets. Overweight cats are at risk of diabetes, joint problems, and skin diseases.

Fat cat contender

In 2003 a Siamese called Katy from Russia claimed the unofficial record for heaviest cat, weighing in at 50 lb. (23 kg) with a waist measurement of 27.5 in. (70 cm). "She doesn't really eat that much," her owner asserted, providing a lavish supply of fish, meat, sour cream, and sausages to ward off starvation—not a recommended diet!

Longest cat

The average adult male cat is 28–29 in. (71–73 cm) long, including tail, which gives some idea of the size of a Maine Coon called Leo, resident in Chicago who currently holds the record for the longest cat. Leo measures a magnificent 48 in. (122 cm) from nose to tail—as long as an eight-year-old child.

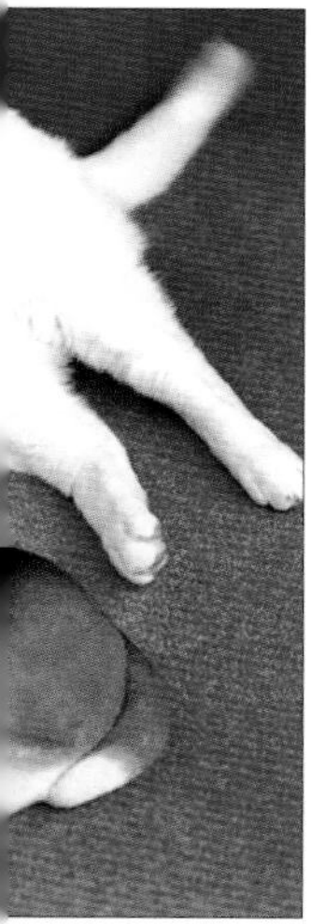

In 1988 Garfield from Denmark achieved the dubious honor of being the fattest cat in Europe. Overfeeding any pet to this degree is ill advised, causing health problems and shortening lifespan.

Snowbie of Aberdeenshire was a previous holder of the title of Longest Cat. In 1997, aged four, he measured 40.5 in. (103 cm) from nose to tail tip.

Smallest cat

The smallest cats on record include Tinker Toy, a blue-point Himalayan from Illinois (2.75 in./7 cm high and 7.5 in./19 cm long), Itse Bitse (3.75 in./9.7cm high and 15 in./38 cm long), and tabby Mr. Peebles (6.1 in./15.5 cm high and 19.2 in./48.8 cm long). These all appear to be the result of natural mutations.

A convincing fake

A dramatic photograph currently making the rounds purports to be that of giant "mutant cat" Snowball, said to weigh 87 lb. (39.5 kg) as a result of exposure to atomic radiation. The story behind the picture is less fantastic: American Cordell Hauglie created it as a family joke, photo-editing a picture of his normal cat Jumper on his computer, and was surprised to see it circulating on the Internet with a fake caption. Some still believe it!

BLACK CATS

Phoenician fancy

Black cats have a long history. They were probably the first color variety to arise from the ancestral tabby. This mutation is thought to have originated in the eastern Mediterranean during the classical period, and to have been spread by Phoenician traders. Today the highest concentration of black cats is in Britain and northwest Africa, closely followed by the Mediterranean region, Rome, and Florence.

Black but comely

The spread of the black mutation may have been caused by its novelty value, but there is some evidence that it may also have had a friendlier nature. When a

With his shiny "patent leather" coat, the Bombay was bred to resemble a miniature black panther.

species is domesticated, color mutations often accompany breeding for a tamer temperament, and to this day black cats are often said to be less aggressive, less timid, and more laid-back than the ancestral striped tabby.

Black cats often suit artistic designs, as in this elegant Japanese stamp.

Shades of black

Not all black cats are black. Genetically all cats are tabbies under their apparent color, and often black kittens (and some adults) show "ghost" tabby markings. Black cats exposed to sunlight often fade to brown ("rust"). Furthermore, among pedigree cats, black is not always called black. In Oriental cats it is termed ebony, and in color-points it is termed seal.

Blacklisted

It was unlucky to be a black cat in the Middle Ages, for they were held to be agents of Satan and witches' familiars, to be killed or tormented with the full approval of the church. In fact, they were under attack from both sides. Persecuted in the name of God, they also suffered at the hands of devil worshippers, who believed that sacrificing black cats to Satan could bring them magical powers.

The angel's mark

Medieval persecution of black cats may account for the scarcity of totally black cats (other than pedigrees bred specifically for pure color). It was pure black cats that were considered Satan's own: a patch of white was an "angel's mark" signifying innocence, giving a better chance of survival and of passing on genes to their descendants.

Lucky black cats

The Satanic connection had its upside: some people preferred not to risk offending an animal with such powerful connections, and in English folklore black cats came to be considered bringers of good luck. King Charles I certainly believed this. He treasured his lucky black cat, and may not have been surprised that his arrest by Parliamentary troops, leading to his execution, occurred the day after the cat died.

A survey in 2001 suggests that black cats can be unlucky for some, being four times as likely as paler cats to cause allergies in humans.

Horror story

In Edgar Allan Poe's classic horror story *The Black Cat* (1843), the tortured narrator, descending into alcoholism, kills his once-beloved black cat, Pluto, then later kills his wife. He walls up her body in the cellar, but accidentally entombs Pluto's successor with her, and the cat's cries betray him to the police. Poe himself was a great cat lover, and the tale was inspired by his adored Catarina—a tortoiseshell.

Anarchy

In the 20th century the black cat was adopted as a symbol *(above left)* by the anarchist wing of the labor union movement. The design, by socialist activist Ralph Chaplin, depicts a snarling cat with arched back, bottlebrush tail, and bared claws, and is nicknamed the "wildcat" in reference to wildcat strikes. Its popularity led to wide usage of the name "Black Cat" by anarchist-affiliated groups across Europe.

Russia's national breed, the semi-longhaired Siberian, comes in the full range of colors, including this striking black variety.

WHITE CATS

Eastern princesses

The first recorded litter of purebred white kittens was born in A.D. 999 in the Imperial Palace at Kyoto, Japan. The cat-loving Emperor Ichijo was delighted, and ordered the kittens to be tended like princesses.

The enchanted cat

A famous feline fairy story is *The White Cat*, told in 1682 by the Comtesse d'Aulnoy. A king sets his three sons a series of quests to find who deserves his throne, and a beautiful white cat who lives like a queen in her own palace aids the youngest son to win each quest. At last, she asks the prince to reward her by cutting off her head and tail. Horrified, he refuses, but finally obeys. This breaks the enchantment that made her a cat and turns her back into a princess—and of course they live happily ever after.

Whiter than white

Not all white cats are really white. Some that appear sparkling white at first glance actually have coats ticked with color. Chinchilla cats have silver hairs with color at the very tips, and Suqutranese have white hairs banded with silver, in both cases creating a glittering "whiter than white" effect. The villain Blofeld's famous white cat in the James Bond films was played by a spectacular Chinchilla called Solomon.

Floury camouflage

White cats were once known as "millers' cats." They were favored as mousers by millers, as it was believed that the mice would find it harder to spot a white cat among the flour bags.

White Jewel

One of the rarest white breeds is the Khao Manee from Thailand, treasured in its native land where it is nicknamed the White Jewel or Diamond Eye. A pure white shorthair, it is notable for its glowing eyes, which may be blue, green, or yellow but are ideally of different colors (one blue and one yellow eye being valued as the "gold and silver eye cat"). Some say this, rather than the Siamese, is the true royal cat of old Siam.

◂◂ *Two contrasting white breeds, an odd-eyed White British Shorthair and a blue-eyed White Persian, with little in common but their snowy fur*

Partially white cats	
White markings	**are called**
Mainly white with a few patches of color	**Harlequin** or **Magpie**
50 percent white	**Bicolor**
White with color on head, tail, and sometimes legs	**Van pattern**
White with colored back extending to ears and top of head like a hooded cape	**Mask** and **mantle**
As above, but with a break between back and head coloring	**Cap** and **saddle**
White paws	**Mitts** or **Gloves**
Small white patch on chest	**Locket**
Row of white patches on belly	**Buttons**
White paws, belly, chin, optional tail tip	**Tuxedo**

White British Shorthairs may have gold, copper, deep sapphire blue, or odd (mismatched) eyes.

One blue eye and one gold give the odd-eyed White a particularly striking appearance.

TABBY CATS

Wild silk

The beautifully marked tabby takes its name from a kind of watered silk known as tabby *(attabi)* after the Attabiyah district of Baghdad where it was made. Tabby is the oldest color in cats, inherited from their wild ancestors. Made up of areas of striped hairs alternating with areas of solid-colored hairs, it forms a pattern as complex and delicate as any created by the Baghdad silk weavers.

A brown mackerel British Shorthair shows the typically striped markings of this variety.

Signed edition

Many tabbies have a clear "M"-shaped marking on the forehead. Islamic legend says this is the signature of Mohammed, who marked his blessing on his tabby cat Muezza after it saved his life by killing a snake that crawled up his sleeve. In Christian legend, it is the signature of the Virgin Mary, who blessed the cat for curling up in the manger to keep the baby Jesus warm.

The "M"-shaped mark on the forehead of tabby cats has a benevolent significance in both Islamic and Christian religious traditions.

Original stripes

Striped or mackerel tabbies are adorned with thin stripes and rings in a "fishbone" pattern. This is the original tabby design, inherited from the African Wildcat ancestor. Markings include banded legs and tail, a double row of "vest buttons" along the stomach, and one or more "necklaces" around the chest.

Imperial blotches

Blotched or classic tabbies have thicker stripes and whorls spread out into blotches, ideally forming "bull's-eyes" on the sides and a "butterfly" on the shoulder. This pattern is a mutation thought to have arisen in 16th-century Britain (and separately in northeastern Iran). British ships spread blotched tabby cats around the world, and their present distribution reflects the spread of the British Empire.

A beautifully elegant spotted tabby—in this case a Cameo Tabby Oriental Shorthair.

Stunning spots

Geneticists can't decide whether spotted tabbies are a variation on striped tabbies with the stripes broken up into spots or the result of a separate spotting gene. The oldest spotted breeds, the Spotted British Shorthair and Egyptian Mau, both developed naturally. More recently, breeders created the Ocicat and Australian Mist, and later produced other spotted breeds such as the Bengal by hybridization with wild species.

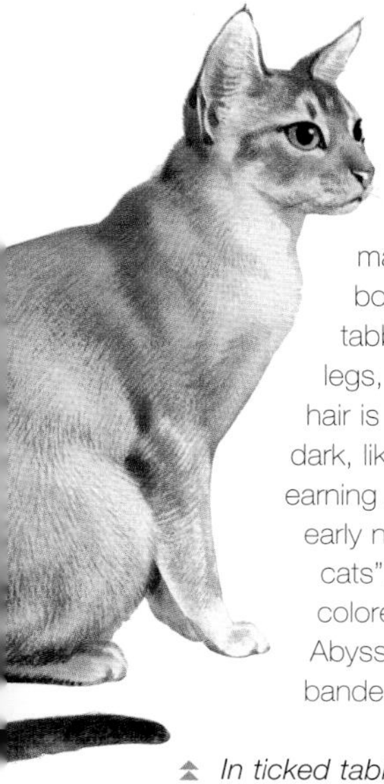

In ticked tabbies, such as this Blue Abyssinian, each hair is distinctively marked with lighter and darker bands of color.

Tabbies in disguise

Ticked tabbies don't look like tabbies at all, because they lack markings on their bodies (they may have tabby markings on the legs, face, and tail). Each hair is banded in light and dark, like a wild rabbit's—earning Abyssinians the early nickname of "bunny cats". Not all are rabbit colored: sorrel Abyssinians have hairs banded in apricot and dark brown, and Singapuras have delicate ivory and sepia banding.

Sorrel Abyssinians display a rich coppery red color ticked with chocolate.

Colors

Tabbies come in more than 40 color varieties, including brown tabby (brown, black markings), blue tabby (pale blue-gray, slate-blue markings), red tabby (rich or pale orange, darker orange markings), and even cinnamon, chestnut, and lavender tabbies. So-called red cats are really red tabbies with minimal contrast between ground color and tabby markings—but close examination gives away their secret.

MARMALADE AND TORTOISESHELL

Tabbies in disguise

To the geneticist they are orange; to cat lovers they are ginger, red, yellow, or marmalade. Under any name, ginger cats are the most brightly colored variety. To date, though, there are no true reds or oranges among cats: they are all really tabbies, though selective breeding has increased the red coloring and reduced the tabby markings until in some cases they are barely visible.

Blue tortoiseshells like this Scottish Fold display pastel hues.

The tabby markings on marmalade cats vary from bold to faint, but are always present.

Viking rovers

Ginger cats were evidently the Vikings' favorite. Although the red color mutation probably first occurred in Asia, today's distribution of ginger cats across northern Europe leads geneticists to believe that they were distributed by Viking voyagers. Many Vikings settled in Scotland, in particular the western islands, which to this day have a particularly high concentration of ginger cats.

Pretty in patchwork

Brilliant colors are also to be seen in tortoiseshell cats (black and red) and tortoiseshell-and-whites (also known as calico or chintz, after the gaily patterned fabrics). Less well known but equally attractive are the pastel versions created by color dilution genes, lightening red to cream and black to blue (gray), lilac, or chocolate.

Lucky colors

Tortoiseshell cats are regarded as lucky in many countries, including Scotland, Ireland, and Canada. In Japan, tortie-and-whites, known as Mi-ke ("three-furred") are considered particularly lucky. Japanese fishermen

A handsome tortie-and-white Persian in glowing colors.

liked to have Mi-ke cats aboard, believing they would protect boats from storms—and the crew from ghosts.

In Stephen Elmer's painting of Selima's demise (c.1776) he includes a volume open at Gray's Ode *on her death to identify the scene.*

Tortie elegy

Famous torties include Selima, beloved pet of Horace Walpole (1717–97). Her accidental death in 1747 was commemorated in Thomas Gray's *Ode on the Death of a Favourite Cat, Drowned in a Tub of Gold Fishes.* "I am about to immortalize [her] for one week or fortnight," Gray informed the bereaved Walpole, but his gently ironic elegy has preserved her memory much longer.

Sex discrimination

It is popularly believed that all tortoiseshell cats are female. This is untrue—about one in 3,000 torties is male—but then again it is also true, because male torties are not true males. Tortie coloring requires two X (female) chromosomes, and males have one X and one Y (male) chromosome. Tortie males, therefore, owe their color to a genetic mistake, such as an extra X chromosome and are usually sterile.

Color and temperament

Several surveys examining possible links between color and temperament have found a widespread belief that tortoise-shell cats are generally mischievous—"naughty torties." However, opinions of ginger cats differ considerably: some consider them friendly, others unfriendly.

The famous Morris

Perhaps the most famous ginger cat is Morris, *(below)* an American media star whose cat food advertisements have made him one of the most popular brand icons of all time—when he campaigned for the U.S. presidency in 1988 and 1992, polls showed that only George Bush had better name recognition among voters. The original Morris was rescued from a Chicago animal shelter in 1968; Morris IV took over the role in 2005.

THE REST OF THE RAINBOW

Countless colors

A mere nine basic genes define a cat's color, but modifying genes and gene combinations together produce an astonishing palette of colors, including mink, champagne, peach, platinum, cinnamon, and smoke. Recognized colors and combinations of colors are impossible to number, not least because the same color often has different names in different breeds.

The Korat is always silver-blue, with silver tipping becoming more pronounced with age

Brown study

Pure brown cats (as opposed to brown tabbies) were treasured in ancient Thailand. When first imported to the U.K. in the 19th century (as "Siamese with coats of burnished chestnut with greeny-blue eyes") they lost out to the more striking pointed Siamese, and soon more or less disappeared from the scene. However, more appreciative breeders later revived the color as the Burmese, Tonkinese, and Havana Brown.

Rhapsody in blue

Apart from the villainous Buxton in the animated film *Dougal and the Blue Cat*, blue cats are actually various subtle shades of gray. Blue occurs in several breeds, but three ancient breeds are exclusively blue: the Russian Blue, Chartreux, and Korat. The "blue cat of France," the Chartreux, was once valued by furriers for pelts, but the Russian Blue and Korat were both valued as bringers of good luck to their owners.

Pretty in pink

Cats don't come in a true pink either, but they can be lilac (otherwise known as lavender), a warm dove gray with a definite pinkish tone. In Australia they can also be peach (elsewhere known as fawn), a pinkish cream to fawn shade. The Australian Mist, a spotted or

Two handsome browns: a Brown Burmese and a Havana Brown, also known as Oriental Shorthair.

marbled breed of many subtle colors, occurs in a peach version, described as having pinkish-fawn markings against a cream ground.

Beauty tips

Two-tone hairs with darker tips create subtle color effects. Minimal color at the very tips creates Chinchilla or Shell (longhair) and Tipped (shorthair) breeds with a sparkling appearance. Heavy tipping, with pale color only at the roots, creates "Smokes," which seem solid-colored until the coat ripples with movement. Between the two come "Shaded" breeds with medium tipping. There are also "Goldens," with gold instead of white base color, and "Cameos," whose white hairs have red tips.

This exotic shorthair is a Shaded Cameo, with a mantle of red over a white undercoat.

Albinos in disguise

Typically, albinos are white with pink eyes. Albino cats are different. Pink-eyed Whites are rare, and most feline albinos have blue eyes. However, pointed breeds such as Siamese, with pale bodies and colored "points" (tail, ears, and legs), are also a kind of albino that is temperature dependent, with color restricted to the cooler parts of the body. Hot Siamese acquire more color—a warm home, a fever, or even a leg bandage affect the shade.

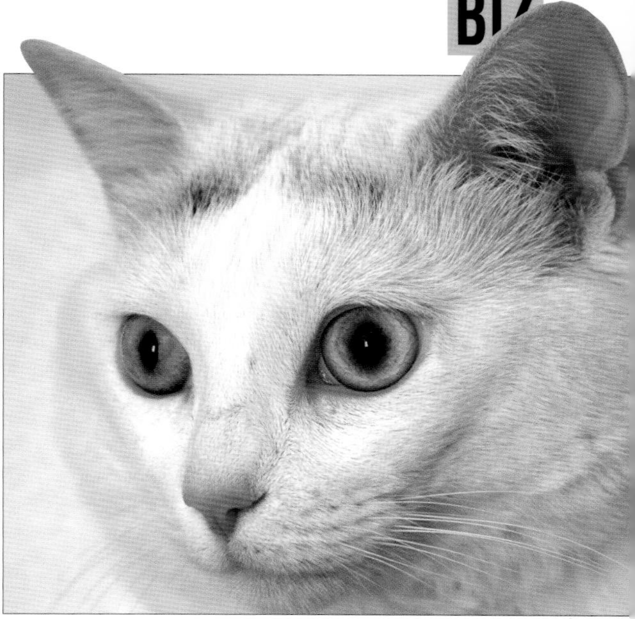

An odd-eyed White with the striking combination of one blue and one green eye.

Eye shades

Cats' eyes can be green, gold, orange, or blue. Random-bred domestic cats tend to have eyes in the greenish-yellow range, but selective breeding of pedigree cats has produced intense colors such as the deep copper eyes of Blue Persians and clear emerald eyes of Chinchillas. Some breeds have eyes of different colors, one blue and one orange or green.

CATS OF THE EAST

Siamese come in different shades. Clockwise from top: seal, lilac, blue, and chocolate point.

Oldest cat book

Well before the West had considered classifying cats into different breeds, the East's cat lovers recognized a range of distinctive types. Indeed, the world's oldest cat book comes from medieval Siam (Thailand). *The Cat Book Poems*, produced some time between 1350 and 1767, is a book of paintings and verses depicting no fewer than 17 breeds, including the Siamese, Copper (forebear of the Burmese), and Korat.

We are Siamese

The Siamese cats of Disney's *Lady and the Tramp* cats sing, "We are Siamese, if you please; We are Siamese, if you don't please"—and when the first Siamese were exhibited in the West, in 1871, they certainly didn't please everybody. Some found them an "unnatural, nightmare kind of cat" and commented that "almost any other cat is pleasanter and safer to live with." Fortunately, others disagreed.

East or West?

The familiar slinky Siamese with its elongated build and long triangular head is not the original Siamese of Thailand, but the result of Western breeders taking the slender "foreign" build to extremes. Early Siamese were chunkier, less exaggerated cats. Today, alongside the "ultra" show type, the old-style Siamese is being revived, known variously as the apple-headed, traditional, or Thai Siamese.

Relative colors

Yellow-eyed, rich brown Burmese (now available in other colors) and blue-eyed, color-pointed Siamese both owe their appearance to a "color restriction" gene allied to albinism. The two breeds represent opposite extremes of the same color spectrum. Crossing Burmese and Siamese produces cats of an intermediate "mink" color range, now classed as a breed in their own right, the Tonkinese.

Copper confusion

Although the Burmese is identified with the "copper cat" of the *Cat Book Poems*, its introduction to the West was confused. Early imports were considered to be brown Siamese, and the breed was actually established from a female, Wong Mau, who was found to be a cross between Siamese and a "new" brown breed—in fact a Tonkinese.

Cloud-colored cats

Another breed from Thailand is the Korat, a

silver-blue beauty described in the *Cat Book Poems* as having fur "with roots like clouds and tips like silver" and eyes "like dewdrops on the lotus leaf." In its native land it is known as the Si-Sawat after the gray Sawat nut, but also as the "good luck cat," a traditional wedding gift held to bring wealth, rain for the crops, and a happy marriage.

This maneki-neko figurine holds a gold coin symbolizing wealth and good fortune.

Beckoning Cat

Japan's "lucky" cat is the *maneki-neko* or Beckoning Cat, nowadays identified with the Japanese Bobtail. Legend says that a rich samurai followed a cat that beckoned him with its paw toward Gotoku-ji temple. A moment later, the spot where he had been standing was struck by lightning. The grateful Samurai became the temple's patron, and the image of the beckoning cat is to this day a popular talisman.

Mysterious drain cat

A small cat the hue of old ivory, the Singapura became known in the 1970s as a native to Singapore, nicknamed the "drain cat" because it sheltered in the city drains. However, it has also been claimed that the breed was manufactured in the U.S. from Burmese and Abyssinians. Whatever the truth, since 1991 it has been the official symbol of Singapore under the name of Kucinta, the Love Cat.

Left: red and lilac tortie Burmese. Right: natural mink and champagne mink Tonkinese.

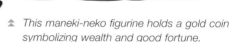

LONGHAIRS

Origins

The cat's wild ancestors were shorthaired. The only long-haired wildcat, Pallas's Cat, is no longer considered to have introduced long coats into the domestic cat. When and where the Longhair gene originated is unknown, though it may have developed first in Russia. Longhairs were unknown in the West until the 16th century, when they were introduced from Turkey and Persia.

Pampered Persians

Persian Longhairs, with stockier build, shorter heads, and longer coats, were imported from Iran, but until the mid-19th century cat lovers did not distinguish between Persians and Angoras and interbred the two. Persian characteristics have been steadily emphasized to create the modern ultra-stocky, flat-faced breed with its luxuriant coat—and also exaggerated types such as the muzzleless Peke-faced Persian.

Proud beauties: tortoiseshell and blue-cream Persians.

Admired Angoras

Italian traveler Pietro della Valle (1566–1652) brought some of the first Angora cats from Turkey to the West. These "ash-coloured, dun and speckled [cats], very beautiful to behold" were fashionable pets for two centuries, but were then supplanted by fluffier Persians. By the 20th century, Angoras were almost extinct outside their native land, but in recent years they have regained popularity.

"Natural" longhairs

Fluffy semi-longhairs like the Maine Coon, Siberian, and Norwegian Forest Cat, with dense but not exaggerated coats, developed naturally as an adaptation to cold climates. Nobody knows whether they derive from a natural mutation or from crossbreeding between local cats and imported longhairs, but the survival of the furriest in each case led to a distinctive native breed.

Refrigerator cats

In 19th-century Pittsburgh, pest-control cats working at refrigeration plants developed over several generations into long-haired "Eskimo cats," adapted to the cold with long, dense coats, bushy tails, and tufted ears. In the chilly conditions where they lived, the longhair gene proved a vital survival asset. Perhaps if the strain had been perpetuated, we would see "refrigerator cats" on the show circuit today.

Less luxuriantly furred than Persians are this white Angora (top) and seal point Birman.

This enchanting ball of fluff will grow up to demand a great deal of regular grooming.

Variants
Several short-haired breeds have developed long-haired versions. Longhairs that cropped up occasionally in Abyssinian, Siamese, or Manx litters were once considered undesirable but today have given rise respectively to the Somali, Balinese, and Cymric breeds. In other cases, deliberate crosses were made to introduce the longhair gene, as in the Burmalayan (Burmese cross Himalayan).

Temple cats
Color-pointed, white-socked Birmans are said to have been the sacred cats of Burma. Legend says that the once-white cats of Khmer temple acquired their beautiful color after the high priest's soul passed into the keeping of his cat Sinh. It was long suspected that both breed and legend were manufactured in France, but the discovery in 1960 of indisputable Birmans at a Tibetan temple may support the official history.

Special needs
Although short-haired cats are equipped to care for their own coats, longhairs are not. Daily brushing is essential to prevent mats and tangles, which, if neglected, may become so bad that the whole coat has to be shaved off. Tangles aren't just unsightly: they are uncomfortable and eventually lead to painful skin problems, so don't consider a longhair unless you are prepared to look after its coat.

HYBRIDS

Nonexistent squittens

"Squittens," supposed cat-squirrel hybrids, occur only in folklore and urban myth: hybridization between two such different species is impossible. The legend probably arose from the occasional occurrence of cats with stunted forelegs caused by a condition termed "radial hypoplasia." Unable to use their forelegs normally, such deformed cats adopt a squirrel-like posture when sitting up with forepaws dangling.

This cat is a loving foster mother to an orphan squirrel, but the two species cannot interbreed.

...and mythical cabbits

Cat-rabbit hybrids ("cabbits") don't exist either. This myth is also linked with hypoplasic cats, whose stunted forelegs make them hop like rabbits, but was originally inspired by the Manx breed, whose long legs and high rumps give them a distinctly rabbity gait. An 1845 history of the Isle of Man states firmly that Manx cats are the offspring of female cats and buck rabbits.

A Coon Cat by name, but not by nature—this handsome breed owes nothing to the raccoon

Raccoon cats

The Maine Coon Cat was thought to be a cat-raccoon hybrid, its large size, dense fur, and bushy tail being ascribed to raccoon blood. In fact, the breed developed naturally in a harsh climate that favored big, strong, shaggy cats, but the name survives. The original "coon cats" were raccoon-colored brown tabbies, other colors being known as Maine Shags, but today all colors come under the same name.

Japanese favorites

Cabbits are popular in Japanese animated films, fluffy bunny-kittens being a perfect concept for anime's cute stylization. Animé cabbits are innocent, friendly creatures who support main characters. Among the most popular are Ryo-Oh-Ki, a cuddly carrot eater who transforms when necessary into an armed spaceship, and Mokona, the bouncy, smiling mascot of the Magic Knights.

Wildcat crosses

Squirrel, rabbit, and raccoon crosses may be out, but domestic cats can hybridize with small wildcat species. New breeds based upon such crosses include the Chausie (Jungle Cat hybrid), Bengal (Leopard Cat hybrid), and Safari Cat (Geoffroy's Cat hybrid), designed to combine exotic appearance and domestic temperament—though it takes several generations to achieve the right combination.

The Bengal combines the markings of the wild Asian Leopard Cat with a gentler nature.

Chromosome complications

One difficulty when hybridizing cat species is that they may have different numbers of chromosomes, which can lead to sterile male offspring. Breeding Safari Cats is problematic for this reason: the Geoffroy's parent has 36 chromosomes, the domestic parent 38. First-generation Safaris have 37 chromosomes, producing larger size, but subsequent generations tend to revert to the domestic scale.

Legends and "mysteries"

The race to produce new exotic cat breeds fueled some unlikely claims. The lynxlike PixieBob was initially claimed to be a bobcat hybrid, and when this was disproved was said to derive from "legend cats," feral cats claimed to have bobcat blood. Other breeders have claimed to produce hybrids with "mystery cats," the unidentified black cats of cryptozoology, but these are apparently just ordinary black cats.

Size problems

The Savannah Cat is the product of hybridization between domestic cats and Servals—a real challenge, as the Serval has to be persuaded to accept a mate only a quarter his size, with a different smell and courtship ritual. Differences in kitten size and gestation period also create problems. This rare breed remains confined to the U.S.

A big-eared, long-legged, medium-sized African wildcat, the Serval is one of many species threatened by the fur trade.

CAT SHOWS

How shows began

The first cat show on record was as early as 1598, but this was only a fair sideshow, with prizes for the best ratter and best mouser. Cat shows as we know them—beauty shows based on breed standards—were a 19th-century creation. The 1860s saw a few small shows in both Britain and the U.S., but the first major cat show to foreshadow the modern system was held at London's Crystal Palace in 1871.

Harrison Weir's aim was to raise the status of an underappreciated species. He succeeded beyond his wildest dreams! He is depicted here with some of the prize cats entered in the 1871 Crystal Palace Show.

The founder

Journalist and artist Harrison Weir (1824–1906) is credited with founding cat shows. Passionately fond of cats, he organized the 1871 show at Crystal Palace to celebrate his favorites and encourage appreciation of the different breeds, colors, and markings. Weir was amazed as well as gratified by the public response. The show was packed, and was to become an annual event.

The founding show

That 1871 show offered 25 classes, with categories including Eastern (Angora, Persian), other Foreign (Russian, Siamese), and British (shorthairs, Manx) varieties, as well as novelty classes such as Biggest Cat and Fattest Cat. The 170 entrants included a genuine Scottish wildcat, too fierce to be handled, and the 54 prizewinners included Weir's 14-year-old tabby, The Old Lady.

Crufts for cats

The name of Crufts is irrevocably associated with the world's most famous dog show. Less widely known is the fact that there was once (twice, actually) a Crufts Cat Show. In 1894, three years after his first dog show, Charles Cruft scheduled a 74-class Great International Cat Show, and did it again the following year. Both shows, though well attended, lost money, and thereafter Cruft stuck with dogs.

Breed development

Harrison Weir had to invent a standard for judging cats. Classing them by shape, color and fur length, he drew up guides that he called Standards of Points (later to evolve into our detailed modern breed standards). In so doing, he may be said to have created the pedigree cat—a development he lived to regret, commenting ruefully that fashionable breeds were in the spotlight at the expense of ordinary household pets.

This G.C.C.F. (Governing Council of the Cat Fancy) catalog lists 1953 show entrants and breeders.

Cat clubs

Since 1887, when the National Cat Club was formed in London, cat shows and pedigree cat breeding have been organized and overseen by various societies and governing bodies. In Britain, it is the Governing Council of the Cat Fancy (founded in 1910), which registers pedigree cats and schedules shows. In the U.S., some six cat associations carry out these functions, the largest being the Cat Fanciers' Association.

Champions and Premiers

These are titles awarded to top show winners, the title of Champion being reserved for un-neutered cats and Premier for neuters. They are achieved by winning three Challenge/Premier Certificates in breed classes. Titled cats can then compete for Grand Champion/Premier Certificates, needing three of these to become a Grand Champion or Grand Premier.

Household pets

Cat shows are not just for pedigrees. Classes for household pets are open to unregistered cats with at least one unregistered parent, often divided by color and/or coat length. Some entrants may be purebred, others mixed-breed, but all are judged not by a standard of points but on condition and temperament. Judges look for healthy, happy, friendly cats—in fact for ideal pets.

Judged on health and temperament, mixed-breeds have their time in the limelight at cat shows, too.

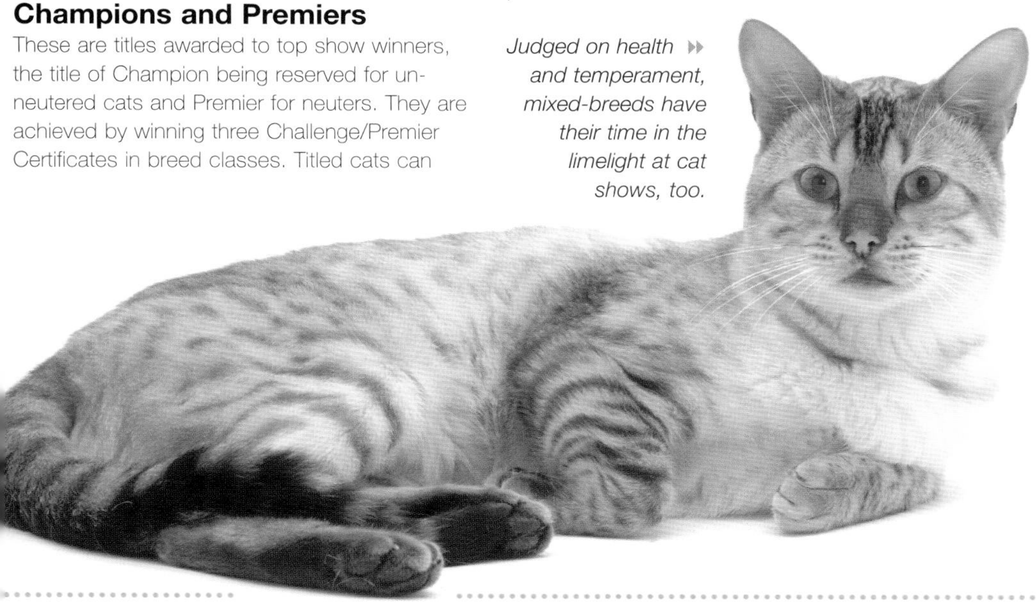

CAT GYMNASTICS

Elastic skeleton

The cat is a natural contortionist, with a supple skeleton designed to stretch and twist. The vertebrae making up its backbone are much more loosely connected than ours, giving the spine its incredible flexibility. Highly mobile shoulder blades give the forelegs more freedom of movement than our arms, and a minimalized collarbone allows the cat to compress its body to fit the tiniest space.

Natural sprinters

A supple backbone is the secret of the cat's speed, which can reach 31 mph (50 kph). Alternately stretching and compressing the spine as it runs extends the cat's running stride to propel it some three times its own length at each step. This is a high-energy technique, so cats are sprinters, not long-distance runners.

Climbing

Climbing comes naturally to cats, with crampon claws and flexible ankle joints that let them descend either headfirst or backward. In the 1940s, a black cat called Mincha climbed a 40 ft. (12-m) tree in Buenos Aires and stayed there for six years, raising three litters in the treetop. But cats don't only climb trees. In 1980 a Yorkshire cat managed to scramble more than 70 ft. (21 m) up a vertical stucco wall!

Cats just can't resist climbing trees, but sometimes they need help to get down.

High-jump champions

Cats can jump five times their own height or more—the equivalent of a human leaping from the ground on to a rooftop. Jumping is powered by thigh muscles so powerful that the human equivalent would produce thighs as thick as our waists.

Safe landing

Falling cats usually land on their feet, rotating in midair to face the ground. This "righting reflex"

The flexible backbone helps to power the cat's running stride, making him a high-speed sprinter.

is shown by kittens as young as two to three weeks, and is fully developed by the time they are seven weeks old. Legend says this was a gift granted to cats by Mohammed. The feline record holder for surviving the longest fall was a Florida cat called Andy, who fell from the 16th floor of an apartment building.

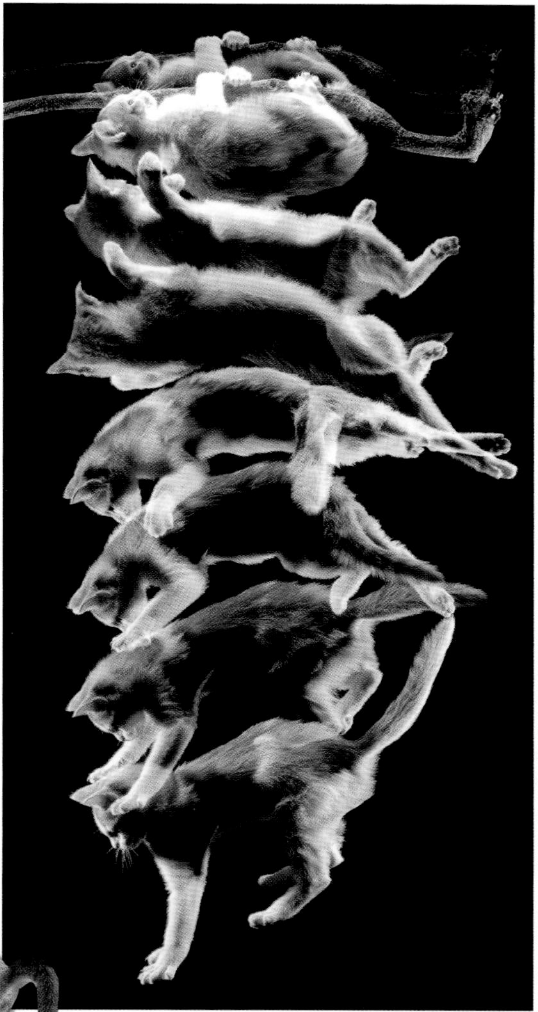

▲ Twisting rapidly in midair, falling cats nearly always land on their feet.

Ordeal by fall

Our medieval ancestors were fascinated by the cat's ability to survive falls, and from 962 to 1817 the Belgian town of Ypres held an annual festival when cats were thrown from the 230-ft. (70-m) Cloth Hall Tower. Amazingly, many of the cats survived. The Ypres Cat Festival is still held today *(right)*, but fortunately now celebrates cats as much-loved pets—since 1817 only toy cats take the plunge from the tower.

Agility tournaments

A new sport in the U.S. is the Cat Agility Tournament, in which cats learn to negotiate an agility course designed to display their speed, coordination, movement, physical condition, intelligence, and training—as well as their relationship with their owner-trainers. In 2005 a Bengal cat named Zoom won the world's first Agility Cat Excellent title.

THE TALE OF THE TAIL

Balancing pole

A cat's tail is a balancing aid. Walking along the top of a fence, the cat maintains its center of gravity by adjusting the position of its tail—just as a tightrope walker uses a pole. Scientists who trained cats to cross a narrow beam observed that when the beam wobbled sideways, the cats instantly swung their tails in the opposite direction to keep their balance—but tailless cats tended to fall off.

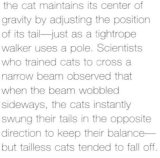

A cat relies on its tail for its phenomenal sense of balance.

Completely tailless Manx cats are colloquially known as rumpies!

How long?

The average cat's tail is 10 in. (25 cm) long and is made up of 21–23 vertebrae, linked together like a string of beads. However, nonaverage cats may have tails ranging from 8 to 14 in. (20 to 36 cm), stumpy tails, or even no tail at all.

No tail

The Manx breed is famous for lacking a tail—legend says that two cats were the last beasts to board Noah's Ark, and that Noah accidentally shut their tails in the door. Although only tailless Manx can be shown, some are born with tails, and these are essential for breeding. Kittens that inherit more than one gene for taillessness die before birth, so every living tailless Manx carries a hidden gene for a full tail.

Some cats have tails that extend well over 1 ft. (30 cm) in length.

Curtailed

Cats with abbreviated tails have cropped up from time to time around the world. Best known is the Japanese Bobtail, which can be traced back to the sixth century, whose few tail-bones kink, curve, or angle to form a pompom bunny tail. No two Japanese Bobtails have identical tails—they are as individual as human fingerprints. A more recent breed, the American Bobtail, has a stubby one-third-length tail reminiscent of a bobcat.

Telling Tails	
Tail position	**Meaning**
Down, with tip curving up	**I feel relaxed.**
Slightly raised and curved	**I wonder what that is?**
Up, with tip curving over	**This is interesting.**
Straight up	**Hello, friend—I'm pleased to see you.**
Straight up, quivering	**I like you.**
Still, but tip twitching	**I am irritated, or perhaps only puzzled.**
Lashing from side to side	**I am very annoyed indeed.**
Straight up, bristling	**(To another cat) I am ready to attack.**
Down, tucked between hind legs	**I'm small and humble and you are the boss.**
Raised, fluffed out	**It's crazy hour—energetic play!**
Down, fluffed out	**I am scared.**

The tail of a Japanese Bobtail is composed of one or more curves in the bone itself, but its structure is hidden by the pompom of tail hair.

Curly tails

Some cats even have curly tails carried over their backs like huskies. Until recently, cats with this genetic mutation were viewed simply as oddities, but in 1999 an American breeder founded a new breed on her curly-tailed kitten. The American Ringtail carries its tail curled when relaxed, but has no loss of tail mobility. Indeed Ringtails are said to make extra use of their tails, curling them around branches when climbing down a tree.

Kinky tails from Malay

Early Siamese cats often had kinked tails, highly prized in their native Thailand but largely bred out in the West, where the tail kink is considered a fault. Tail abnormalities, from kinks to bobtails, are so widespread among the cats of southeast Asia that geneticists believe they originate from a few common ancestors, probably from the Malay peninsula, where the percentage of kinked tails is highest today.

TOOTH AND CLAW

Toothy tool kit

Cats have fewer teeth than any other carnivores, but these are superbly adapted predators' tools. Their canine teeth serve to stab and hold prey, and the molars act as cutlery to cut meat into manageable pieces—cats can't chew their food as we do, but swallow lumps whole. The tiny incisor teeth serve for fine work, plucking feathers or picking meat scraps off bones, and are also used to help comb the cat's fur.

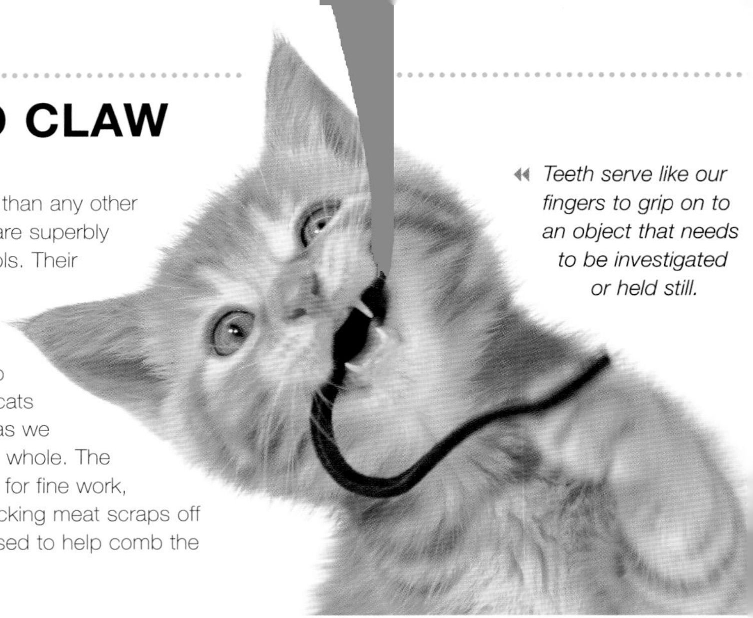

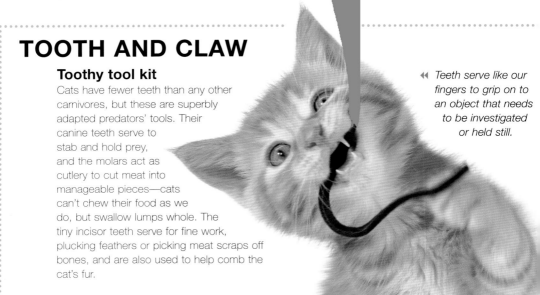

Teeth serve like our fingers to grip on to an object that needs to be investigated or held still.

Hunting daggers

The cat's four long canine teeth (fangs) are highly developed hunting weapons, specifically designed to stab prey in the neck, severing the spinal cord. A large gap behind the canine teeth allows them to be driven in to their full length, and sensitive tissue around them allows the cat to adjust its grip and feel when its fangs are correctly positioned for the kill.

Do cats need dentists?

Surveys suggest that 70 percent of cats over three years old have some degree of dental disease. This is probably caused by the diet we feed them: even the best commercial cat food creates a greater buildup of tartar on teeth than a natural diet of fresh-killed prey. Some cats will allow their owners to clean their teeth with special cat toothpaste; less cooperative felines should have regular dental checkups from the vet.

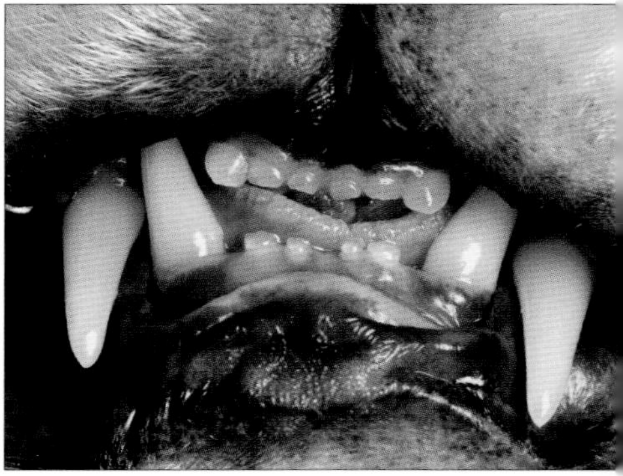

Large canine teeth tackle heavy work, stabbing and gripping, whereas the dainty incisors are geared for more delicate tasks.

Swiss army claws

A cat's claws are as multipurpose as a Swiss army knife. They are hooks, brakes, crampons, combs, and switchblades all in one, designed for climbing, digging, gripping, self-defense, hunting, and fighting. They are also part of the cat's communication system, used to scratch territorial markings or as a visual signal: "Be careful—I'm armed!"

Built-in scabbards

Cats don't waste their super-efficient claws by walking on them. When not in use, their claws are tucked away in skin sheaths on the toes and held in place by elastic ligaments. This is their normal, relaxed position, but cats have only to contract their muscles to send the claws flashing out.

More than a manicure

Cats who are accused of "sharpening their claws" on furniture are not guilty as charged. Feline claws don't need sharpening so much as stripping. They grow in layers, like an onion, and when the outer layer grows worn, scratching rough surfaces such as tree trunks or furniture strips it off to expose a fresh layer. Scratching also serves to place scent marks and to give leg and shoulder muscles a good workout.

Weapons—but not for war

A cat's teeth and claws are effective weapons, so much so that cats try to avoid using them when fighting their own kind. The reason cat fights sound so violent is that they depend more on sound effects than on actual violence. Screeching and glaring can often win a battle without any physical damage to either side.

Claws require regular maintenance—so indoor cats should be supplied with scratching posts, or the furniture will suffer.

Declawing? Don't!

In the U.S. and Canada, cat owners can tackle scratching problems by having their pets declawed. This operation—amputating the first joint of each front toe—is banned in most other countries as an unjustifiable mutilation, and one that is not only painful but damaging. Declawed cats can't damage furniture, but neither can they walk normally (leading to stressed joints and arthritis), climb, dig in a litter box, or defend themselves if attacked.

WHAT BIG EYES YOU HAVE

Eyes front

Vision matters more to cats than to most carnivores—although hearing, smell, and touch matter even more—and they have bigger eyes in relation to their body size than any other mammal. Unlike most carnivores, their eyes face to the front rather than the sides, giving binocular vision like ours and, indeed, a wider visual field than we have (295 degrees compared with 210).

Forward-facing eyes give binocular vision and a wide visual field. Eye color has no bearing on the acuteness of a cat's vision.

A hunter's view

Cats' eyesight is adapted for hunting. Long-sightedness, with good distance vision (up to around 120 ft./36 m) lets them spot prey far off. Poor vision at close quarters doesn't matter, because at this point nose and whiskers take over. Similarly, cats' eyesight is poor on detail (only one-tenth as good as ours) but superb on spotting movement—a cat sees a blade of grass twitch yards away, whereas we would be unaware of it.

Built-in mirrors

Cats can't see in complete darkness, but they can see perfectly well in what looks like total darkness to us, needing only a sixth of the light intensity that our eyes require. This is because a mirrorlike layer of light-reflecting cells (the tapetum) at the back of the eyes amplifies what scraps of light there are. The brilliant shine of cats' eyes in car headlights is achieved by light bouncing off these "mirrors."

"Glow-in-the-dark" eyes reflect light like mirrors to enhance night vision.

Safety inspiration

In 1933, the shine of cats' eyes inspired inventor Percy Shaw (1890–1976) to develop a road safety device, the cat's eye reflector. Patented in 1934, his simple glass and metal studs laid down the center of the road to reflect approaching lights made night driving much safer, especially during the blackout of World

War II. In 1965 Shaw's lifesaving invention earned him an OBE (Order of the British Empire).

Moon eyes

The cat's elliptical pupils are much more efficient at adjusting to different light levels than our round ones. Whereas we have a single circular muscle to adjust pupil size, cats have two shutterlike muscles that act faster and allow greater size variation—so dramatic that ancient peoples identified the changing of cats' pupils from slits to spheres with the waxing and waning of the moon.

Color sense

Cats are not color-conscious. They do have color vision, distinguishing greens and blues perfectly well and reds to a lesser extent. However, they don't seem to make any real use of this—perhaps because by night all objects are gray. Scientists have found it hard to train cats to distinguish between objects on the basis of color, and for practical purposes they may be considered color-blind.

Third eyelid

Cats have an inner, third eyelid (the nictitating membrane or haw) that protects the surface of the eye and helps to keep it moist. Normally inconspicuous, the third eyelid partially closes over the eye when a cat is ill—a cue for a visit to the vet. Oddly enough, the other time that it becomes apparent is in a thoroughly contented cat, as part of a "cat smile."

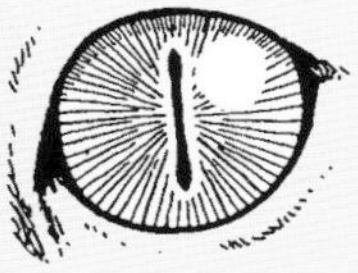

Eye in bright light

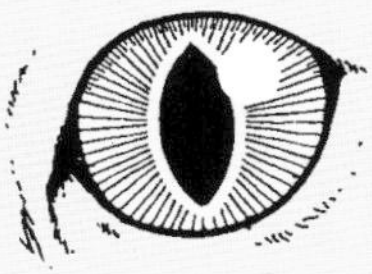

Eye in daylight

Eye in darkness

The cat's pupils adjust to different light conditions far better than ours do, narrowing to mere slits in very bright light.

HEAR HEAR!

Superior ears

Cats' hearing is much better than that of humans, or even of dogs. Ears designed to pick up mouse squeaks can hear sounds at a frequency up to 65 kHz—three times higher than any we can register. They can also hear sounds at a somewhat lower frequency than humans. Cats often respond better to women than to men, and it has been suggested that this is a reaction to the higher-pitched tones of the female voice.

Sound effects

Be careful what music you play in your cat's presence! A Japanese study in which cats' heartbeats were logged while they listened to music revealed that they hated rock, ignored Muzak, but rather liked classical, instrumental, and New Age. Another study in the 1930s found that cats were affected by note E of the fourth octave, which made kittens defecate and adults become sexually excited.

With ears pricked in response to a sound, the cat can locate its source with astonishing accuracy—an essential skill for a hunter.

Satellite dishes

Cats' ears are shaped like cups to direct soundwaves toward the middle and inner ear, and are also remarkably mobile. With 30 muscles to control the movement of each ear, they can swivel 180 degrees toward a sound to detect its precise direction. Tests show that cats can distinguish between two sounds only 18 in. (46 cm) apart at a distance of 60 ft. (18 m).

Folded ears...

Susie, a white farm cat born in Scotland in 1961, had an odd ear mutation that gave rise to the Scottish Fold, a breed with unique ears folded forward and downward, giving an endearing "cloth cap" appearance. Although the ear flap covers the ear opening completely, Scottish Folds have no hearing problems; but the gene is linked with skeletal problems, so Folds are bred to normal-eared cats to avoid these.

American Curl.

Scottish Fold.

...and curly ears

Shulamith, a black longhair born in the U.S. in 1981, demonstrated another mutation—ears curled inward and away from the face, like an imp's horns. She became the founder of the American Curl. Curl kittens are born with normal ears that soon curl up tightly, then gradually relax, reaching the final semi-curved state at about four months. Their eccentric ears seem to work just as well as normal ones.

Very large, high-set ears characterize the curly-coated Cornish Rex, whose breed standard demands deep conical ears.

Feline hearing aid

In June 2003, German acoustics expert Hans-Rainer Kurz announced his invention of a hearing aid for cats. The tiny device can be implanted in the outer ear to enable hearing-impaired cats to pick up sounds that they would never normally distinguish. It cannot help cats that are stone deaf, but for those with severe hearing difficulties it can make a real difference.

Coping with deafness

Deaf cats manage surprisingly well even without hearing aids. They can't hear danger coming, but their other senses of sight, smell, and touch help to compensate. In fact, they "hear" to some extent through their feet and whiskers, picking up sounds in the form of vibrations in the ground and in the air.

THE NOSE THAT KNOWS

Super-smell

Cats have a larger proportion of their brains devoted to scent than we do. They also have 200 million scent-detector cells in their noses, compared with our mere 5 million. That's how much keener a cat's sense of smell is than ours! However, cats don't hunt by nose, as dogs do. They use their sense of smell mainly to investigate food, locate a mate, check for danger, and generally to read what is going on in the world around them.

The cat's nose contains 40 times as many scent detector cells as ours.

Jacobsen's organ

A cat's sense of smell is backed up by an extra sense. An organ in the roof of the mouth, known as Jacobsen's organ, enables them to "taste" scent particles in the air to obtain more detailed information on particularly interesting smells such as sex pheromones. Sucking the smell into the mouth causes a characteristic grimace known as "flehmen"—so a cat making a face is probably engrossed in scent investigation.

Nose and mouth are both tools for scent analysis.

Communication by nose

A language of smell exists between cats, and they have three sets of scent glands, between the toes, under the tail, and on the face with which to "write" messages to each other. Cats mark their world with scent when they scratch trees, when they excrete, and even when they rub their faces against feline or human friends. Cats living in communities mingle scents so they all wear an instantly recognizable "membership badge" of smell.

Communication failure

When cats and humans live together, the fact that only one of the species lives in a world of smell can make for problems. A cat may reject a clean water dish because his nose detects detergent, or feel the need to scratch new furniture so as to cover its worryingly unfamiliar smell with his own scent. Don't blame the cat—it makes sense according to his nose!

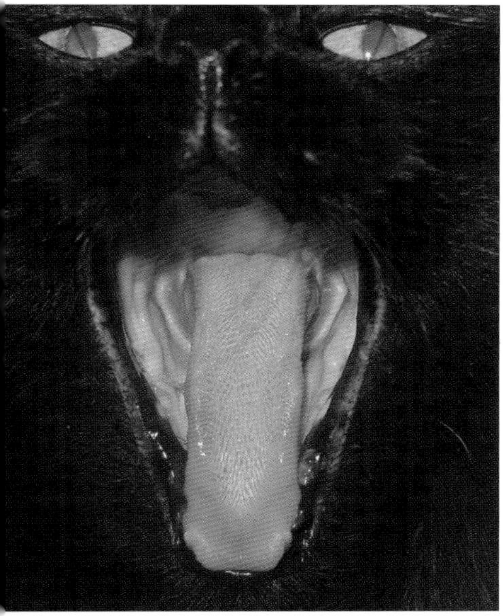

The cat's tongue has a limited array of taste buds, but smell, texture, and temperature are equally important in assessing foodstuffs.

Good taste

The cat's sense of taste is purely utilitarian. We have eighteen times as many taste buds on our tongues as a cat does, enabling us to appreciate the wide range of flavors that go with our omnivorous eating habits. A cat's taste buds are geared to a carnivorous diet, and are limited to detecting meaty and fatty tastes. Genetic analysis has recently shown that cats can't taste sweetness at all.

All food must be checked by nose before a cat will consider eating it. Strong-smelling foods such as tuna are especially attractive.

Food analysis

When it comes to food, cats rely on their sense of smell to tell them what to eat and what to leave. A sick cat with the snuffles and a blocked-up nose often won't risk eating since she can't smell her food. Healthy cats are put off food if it smells wrong, so scrupulously clean food bowls are a must. Older cats whose noses are failing can sometimes be coaxed to eat by warming their meals slightly to heighten the smell.

Customized colors

To pet owners, cats' noses can be pink, reddish, or black. However, nose colors recognized in breed standards include black, seal, brown, chestnut, chocolate, brick red, tile red, cinnamon pink, deep rose, old rose, rose, rosy pink, salmon, flesh, pink, coral pink, lavender pink, lavender, pale fawn, blue, and slate blue. Furthermore, nose prints are as individual as human fingerprints.

WHISKER WISDOM

Super-sensitive

Cats' whiskers are extraordinarily sensitive antennae. They are actually modified hairs, more than twice as thick as normal hairs and with roots three times as deep, richly supplied with nerve endings—as many as we have for our entire hands and fingers. Whiskers provide sensory input not only on anything they touch but also on air currents, enabling the cat to detect the position of both moving and stationary objects.

A sensory network of whiskers surrounds a cat's face, providing detailed information on his surroundings and "reading" air currents.

Whisker layout

Two rows of prominent whiskers on the cheeks, plus smaller whiskers on the muzzle, above the eyes, and also on the wrists, cover most eventualities. Cheek whiskers detect obstacles and measure the space ahead precisely to tell the cat whether she can squeeze through a gap, muzzle whiskers come into their own at close quarters, eye whiskers help to avert eye injuries, and wrist whiskers "watch out" for the paws.

Night "vision"

The sensitivity of the long, prominent cheek whiskers helps the cat to "see" in the dark by registering the least change in air pressure that indicates an obstacle—or prey. They are so efficient that a blind cat can find her way around obstacles using whiskers alone. Researchers have found that sight and whisker "vision" are closely linked in the cat's brain—indeed, if you gently touch a cat's whiskers, her eyes will automatically blink.

Whisker mobility

Specialized muscle attachments allow a cat to direct her whiskers in any direction, and indeed the upper and lower rows of cheek whiskers can move independently. Whiskers need to move only 1/2,000th of the width of a human hair to send signals to the cat's brain.

How long is a whisker?

Generally, the length of a cat's whiskers depends on the size of the cat: they need to be

Whiskers are highly mobile, enabling them to focus upon whatever attracts attention.

Slipping through narrow gaps is made so much easier when whiskers can gauge the exact space available. Never trim your pet's whiskers!

long enough to span the full width of the cat's body in order to assess whether spaces are cat sized or not. The longest whisker on record, belonging to a Maine Coon from Finland, measured 6.8 in. (17.3 cm). Curly-coated Rex cats often have curly whiskers that don't quite fulfil their purpose and tend to break, although no one has studied whether this disadvantages them as a consequence.

Hunting tools

Whiskers are vital tools for hunting. Like a personal radar kit using air movement rather than sound, they detect movement of prey at a distance. At close range a cat's whiskers are much more effective than her eyes, and once the prey is caught the whiskers surround it to tell the cat where to bite and when its dinner is dead. Cats with clipped or damaged whiskers have difficulty killing prey quickly and cleanly.

Whisker talk

Whiskers are also used as part of a cat's body language. Whiskers pointed forward and fanned out indicate interest, excitement, or at least a friendly greeting. Bunched together and flattened to the sides of the face, they indicate a reserved or worried mood. When the cat is relaxed, they spread sideways "in neutral." Cats touch whiskers as part of their greeting ritual to gather information about each other.

A cat's whiskers are more useful than eyes or ears when it comes to close-range hunting.

PAWS FOR THOUGHT

Touchy-feely

Cats' paws are as well equipped with nerves as our hands and fingers, and are extremely sensitive both to touch and to vibration. A cat investigates objects with his paws, but he can also sense the movement of a passing mouse by vibrations through the ground. This refined sense enables deaf cats to "feel" sounds they cannot hear, and also accounts for cats' apparent ability to predict the approach of earthquakes.

What's this? Sensitive paws are the cat's best tools to find out the answer.

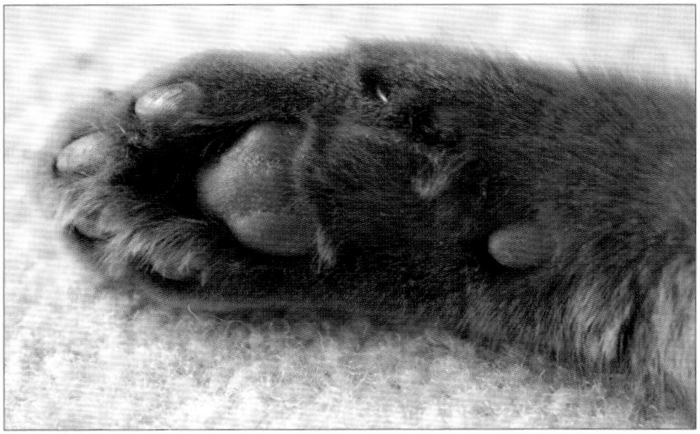

These paws are made for walking—and running, and come with an efficient braking system.

All-terrain boots

Cats' paws combine the sensitivity of fingers with the toughness of hiking boots. The pads have thick "soles" made up of rough skin about 0.05 in. (1.3 mm) thick to provide both protection and a good grip on any surface. A layer of fat acts as an "inner sole" to cushion the foot against impact, and the pads also serve as silencers, enabling the cat to approach prey noiselessly.

Ground control

The paw pads have an anti-skid surface, and also serve as brakes by spreading wide to increase traction when a cat swerves or comes to a sudden halt. The efficiency of this design inspired a leading tire company to develop a "cat's paw" car tire, introduced in 2002, with a tread that widens in the same way when cornering or braking to increase grip and shorten stopping distances.

Flexible fabric

Paws are highly flexible, making superb hunting tools that allow the cat to snatch prey out of the air at astonishing angles. This suppleness also enables the cat to use his paws as cloths to wash behind his ears. Licking the side of his paw to make it damp, he can reach up and backward for a thorough wash. Incidentally, cats are unique in using only the side of the paw for face-washing—other small animals use the whole paw.

When his face needs washing, a cat's paw is an efficient washcloth.

Smelly feet

Fur-coated animals don't have sweat glands over their bodies, where sweat would matt the fur: they have them in their feet instead. The sweat glands in a cat's paws act both as cooling devices in hot conditions and a means of leaving scent messages for other cats. When a cat scratches trees and other marking posts, secretion from these glands acts as territorial graffiti to record his presence.

Southpaws and others

Just as humans are usually right-handed or left-handed, most cats have a dominant paw. In one study, researchers discovered that 38 percent of cats were southpaws, 10 percent favored their right paws, and 40 percent were ambidextrous. Other studies suggest that a lot depends on lifestyle—among indoor cats, whose paw practice is limited because they do not need to hunt, more were found to be right-handers and far fewer were ambidextrous.

Polydactyl cats

Normal cats have 18 toes (four per back paw, five per front). However, polydactyly (extra toes) is not uncommon—the record holder has 28 toes! Polydactyls were once favored as ships' cats, in the belief that extra claws made better mousers. Author Ernest Hemingway kept polydactyl cats at his home in Florida. Today there is a museum that houses a tribe of six-toed "Hemingway Cats" directly descended from his pets.

ET ("Extra Toes") displays seven-toed forefeet. His hind feet have six toes.

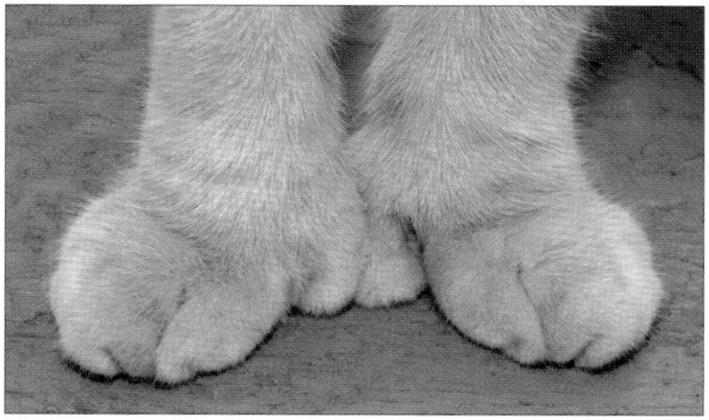

Front feet as massive as boxing gloves don't seem to handicap this polydactyl puss.

A FUR, FUR BETTER THING

Survival gear

A standard shorthair cat wears a three-layered coat—a thermal vest of down hairs next to the skin, then an insulating layer of awn hairs, and finally a topcoat of long guard hairs. With a density of some 60,000 hairs per square inch on the cat's back and twice that number on its underside, fur provides warmth, protection, and camouflage—and a bulletin board to carry scent messages to other cats.

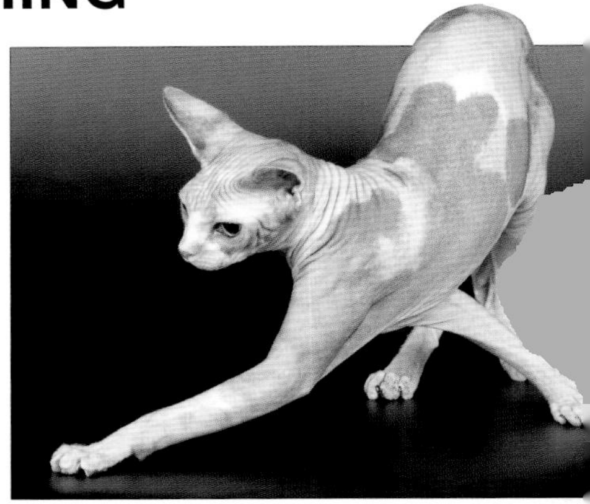

Without the protection of fur, hairless cats like this Sphynx need to be kept indoors.

The cat's fur is a high-tech outfit insulated against heat and cold. It's also pleasurable for humans to stroke—another plus for cats.

Glamour Puss

Long hair occurred in cats as a natural mutation, and selective breeding for increased hair length culminated in the Persian Longhair, with a huge coat created by extra-long guard hairs and extra-thick down hairs. The average modern Persian has fur some 6 in. (15 cm) long, and it has been calculated that, if each hair were laid end to end, they would extend some 230 miles (370 km)!

The Norwegian Forest Cat is geared for a cold climate with his dense insulating coat.

Handsome moderation

Not all longhairs have as much hair as a Persian. Breeds such as the Maine Coon and Norwegian Forest Cat have dense, fluffy coats developed by natural selection to cope with cold climates. Semi-longhairs such as the Somali, Balinese, and Turkish Van have silky coats of intermediate length, usually without the Persian's dense undercoat but adorned with ruff and plumy "squirrel" tail.

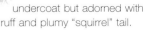

Bald facts

Hairless mutations have occurred several times across the world, but it was not until 1966 that a naked kitten born in Canada gave rise to a bald breed, the Sphynx. A later, different mutation in Russia produced the bald Don Sphynx and Peterbald. Most hairless cats have a sparse "peach-fuzz" down and feel like suede hot water bottles, but the latest discovery, the Hawaiian Hairless, has rubbery skin that lacks even hair follicles.

Hard wired

Adam, a red-and-white kitten with an unusual wiry coat, was born on a New York farm in 1966. Unlike the rex mutation, which has occurred in many countries, the wirehair gene remains unique, and Adam became the founder of the only breed of this type, the American wirehair. The coarse, resilient coat with its lamblike texture is created by extra-thin hairs that are twisted, hooked, or bent—even the whiskers are crimped.

Cats with perms

The Rex breeds have curly coats, often without guard hairs and sometimes even with curly whiskers. Different mutations have given rise to a number of Rex breeds. Best known are the poodle-coated Cornish Rex and gremlinlike Devon Rex. Longhair Rexes are rarely bred, as the coat is unmanageable, matting into dreadlocks, but semi-longhairs with attractive ringlets occur in, for example, the Selkirk Rex and LaPerm.

The American Wirehair's coat is unique among cats with its coarse, kinky texture.

The soft, curly coat of the Cornish Rex consists almost entirely of short down hairs.

Shedding

Wildcats shed twice a year, changing from winter coat to summer coat and back again. The key factor is the amount of sunlight: more light signals time to shed the winter coat, whereas less light suggests that the summer coat needs replacing. Centuries of living in sheltered accommodation have changed domestic cats' shedding schedule, so most shed lightly all year-round—though diet, heredity, and stress also influence shedding.

CATS AND CATNIP

What is catnip?

Catnip *(left)* is an herb belonging to the mint family. It has long been famous for its appeal to cats—in fact, its Latin name of *Nepeta cataria* can be loosely translated as "cats' herb." Native to Eurasia, it is often cultivated in cat-lovers' gardens and has also been introduced to the U.S., where it grows wild. As well as attracting cats, its leaves have been used for herbal teas, medications, and a poultice for bruises.

A catnip mouse is a favorite toy, though kittens under three months old are not yet sensitive to the herb.

A legal "high"

Catnip contains a chemical called nepetalactone to which many cats are sensitive, reacting with a harmless, short-term, and evidently enjoyable intoxication. Cats roll in catnip, rub themselves against the leaves, and chew them, becoming "high" on the effect for a few minutes or sometimes up to an hour or so. Catnip has been described as a nonaddictive, legal recreational drug for cats!

Cats react differently to catnip. Some go wild, rolling and leaping about, whereas others "chill out" in a state of complete relaxation.

Uppers and downers

Although catnip generally excites cats, for humans the leaves are more often used as a mild sedative, said to ease headaches and stomach upsets and to soothe colicky babies. Indeed, although when sniffed by a cat the herb acts as an "upper," when taken internally it becomes a "downer" and has a sedative effect.

Varying appeal

Not all cats are crazy about catnip. Sensitivity to nepetalactone depends on a specific gene, which about 20 percent of cats lack. Kittens and elderly cats don't react to catnip anyway: it is thought that the chemical mimics sexual pheromones and thus appeals to cats of reproductive age. Furthermore, not all catnip is the same, depending on varying growing conditions, and some kinds appeal more than others.

Catnip toys

Catnip-stuffed toys are usually popular with cats, although some of those bought in shops have been on the shelves for a while, losing their freshness. Homemade toys using fresh leaves may be more of a success. Over-exposure to catnip reduces a cat's sensitivity to it, so for maximum effect offer a catnip toy only at intervals (say every two or three weeks) to maintain effectiveness.

Making a catnip mouse *(right)*

This is an easy toy to make—and even if your cat is one of those that doesn't react to catnip, she will have fun playing with it.

You will need:
Dried catnip leaves
A baby's sock
Small piece of cardboard
Felt scraps
Darning thread
Darning needle
Scissors

Cut the end of the sock off at the heel, discarding the top to leave a little woolen bag. Cut out a teardrop shape from the cardboard a little smaller than this bag. Insert this into the bag to act as a base, and stuff the catnip on top. Fold back the top of the bag, make a line of running stitches with the darning thread around the edge, then draw it tight to close the bag and tie it off neatly to form the pointed head end. Stitch on felt ears and use the darning wool to create the tail and whiskers.

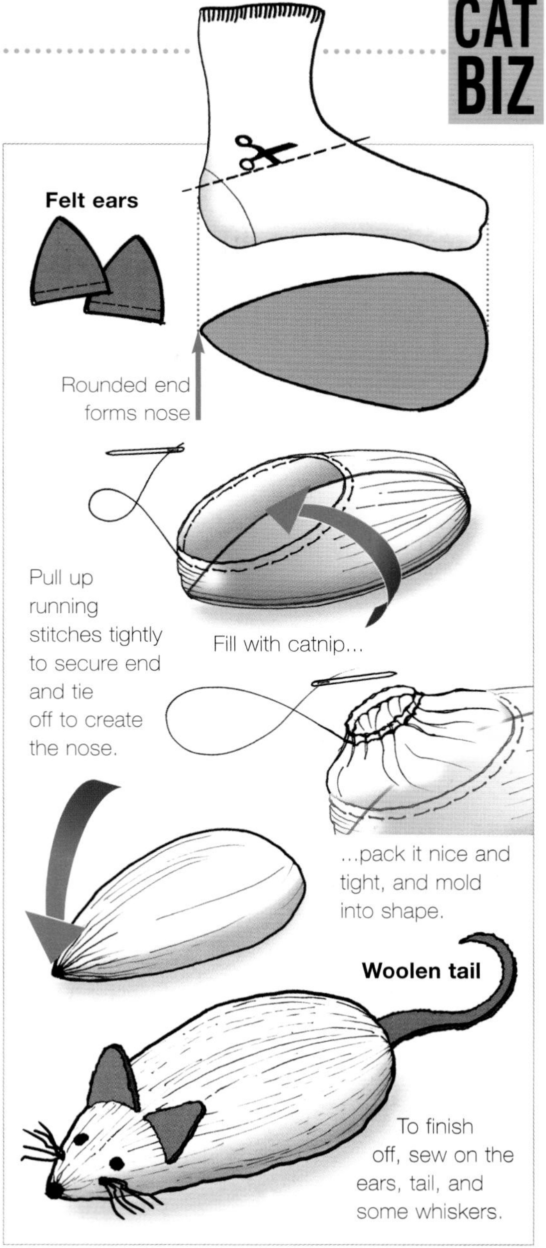
Felt ears
Rounded end forms nose
Fill with catnip...
Pull up running stitches tightly to secure end and tie off to create the nose.
...pack it nice and tight, and mold into shape.
Woolen tail
To finish off, sew on the ears, tail, and some whiskers.

CAT CHAT

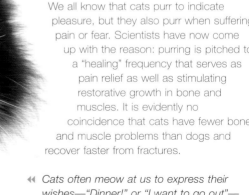

Feline chatterboxes

The domestic cat is one of the most talkative of mammals, able to make more than a hundred different vocal sounds—ten times as many as dogs. How chatty your cat is may depend on its breed. Siamese are famous, even notorious, for the range and quantity of their conversation, whereas Persians and Abyssinians tend to be quiet creatures with little to say.

Meows and more

Cats caterwaul, chatter, chirrup, growl, hiss, purr, scream, yowl, and produce a wide variety of meows. Modern researchers divide cat vocalizations into three groups, vowel sounds (including meows), murmurs (including purring), and high-intensity calls (including open-mouthed wailing, spitting, and hissing). The familiar meow serves mainly to communicate with humans—among wildcats and ferals, it is used only by kittens.

Wordy theories

Eighteenth-century naturalist Dupont de Nemours believed cats spoke a human-style language with distinct words, "a language which has the same vowels as pronounced by the dog, and with six consonants in addition—m, n, g, h, v and f." In the next century Professor Alphonse Leon Grimaldi of Paris took this idea further, claiming to have identified a language with some 600 words, "more like modern Chinese than anything else."

The healing purr

We all know that cats purr to indicate pleasure, but they also purr when suffering pain or fear. Scientists have now come up with the reason: purring is pitched to a "healing" frequency that serves as pain relief as well as stimulating restorative growth in bone and muscles. It is evidently no coincidence that cats have fewer bone and muscle problems than dogs and recover faster from fractures.

◀◀ *Cats often meow at us to express their wishes—"Dinner!" or "I want to go out"—but some just seem to enjoy chatting.*

Body language: the arched back, fluffed-up fur, and bottlebrush tail make this kitten look bigger as part of his threat display.

War cries

Caterwauling, the sinister wailing from outside that wakes us at night, is the vocal expression of aggression between rival tomcats. The threatening sound suggests all sorts of mayhem, but in fact very often it serves as a substitute for a cat fight, with each cat attempting to frighten off its rival without the need for physical violence.

Translating machine

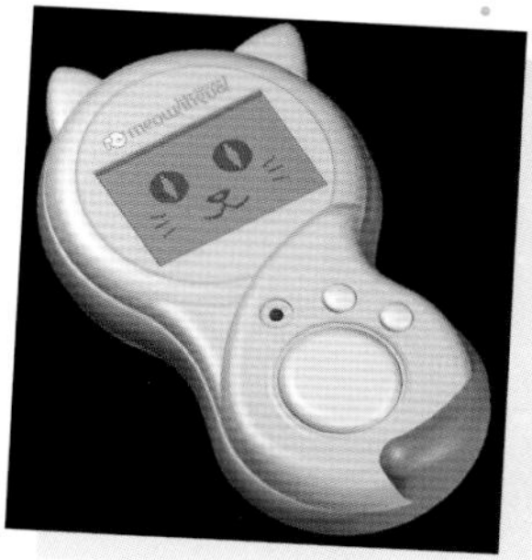

Recently Japanese inventors have come up with the Meowlingual *(right)*, a "feline translation device" to convert meows and purrs into human speech. A successor to the top-selling Bowlingual for dogs, its built-in microphone and voice print analyzer enable it to bring up "translations" on its LCD screen. It also offers body-language analysis, medical analysis—and a feline fortune-telling function.

Even other species can read facial expression when it is written as clearly as this—exposed teeth and narrowed eyes are a clear warning.

Silent speech

Cats communicate with each other not only by voice but by body language, facial expression, and smell. Even a mere human can read a cat's face easily enough. Aggression is signaled with drawn-back ears and slitted pupils, fear by flattened ears, wide pupils, and tightened lips. Contentment produces a relaxed face, with senses turned down low, and a curious cat turns its senses on full, with eyes, ears, and whiskers all alert.

GROOMING

Washday every day

Cats are fussy about cleanliness. They spend one-third of their waking hours grooming themselves, and many also enjoy grooming other cats or even humans within their families. Cats' saliva serves as both soap and water, being a powerful cleaning agent, though unfortunately, like many cleaning agents, it can set off allergies in some humans.

Washing is a soothing activity. In moments of stress, cats wash to calm themselves down.

Homeless and unwashed

Feral city cats often look grubby because they are exposed to more dirt than they can tackle. Cats are equipped to wash off "natural" dirt such as mud and blood, but scavenging alley cats are exposed to greases and chemicals that don't wash out so easily. Furthermore, overcrowding, disease, and food shortages may mean they lack the time and the strength to keep themselves clean.

Why do cats wash?

Washing achieves a great deal more than just keeping fur clean and healthy. It assists temperature insulation: well-kept fur fluffs up better to keep its owner warm on cold days, and on hot days saliva spread over the fur evaporates to act as a coolant. It improves waterproofing, and reinforces scent messages on the fur. Finally, it aids vitamin intake: the cat ingests vitamin D as it licks its fur.

Grooming kit

A cat's tongue is both washcloth and comb. It feels rough, like sandpaper, because it is covered with small, hard, backward-facing

A complete hairdressing kit, the cat's tongue serves to wash, comb, and dry his fur.

Accustoming your cat to being groomed from kittenhood means he will enjoy it as an adult.

barbs termed "papillae," formed of keratin (like our fingernails). They act like a comb's teeth to work through the fur—and big cats such as lions and tigers have tongues so rough they can strip flesh off the bones of prey simply by licking steadily.

Human assistance

Although cats are efficient self-groomers, longhairs need a little help from their friends, and shorthairs usually appreciate this too. Brushing and combing your cat (daily for longhairs, and perhaps twice a week for shorthairs) is a great opportunity for bonding and also for basic cat maintenance, allowing you to check for parasites or any other health problems on a regular basis.

Hairballs

Cats often swallow loose hairs when grooming, and these may collect in the stomach until the cat is really uncomfortable and then be regurgitated as hairballs. Longhairs are particularly prone to this problem. The development of hairballs can be prevented by assisting the cat with grooming, especially during shedding, and there are also specific cat foods and remedies designed to assist.

The cat family that washes together stays together. It's a vital bonding exercise.

Social grooming

Cats groom their friends and families as a bonding exercise. It's a way of displaying mutual affection, and also a means of spreading their personal scents. Cats that live together will carry each other's scent so that they all wear a "family smell," and grooming helps to reinforce this identifying badge. A cat that has been separated from its family will smell wrong to them on its return, needing a great deal of grooming to fit in again.

CATS AND KITTENS

Multiplication

Cats are all too good at multiplication. A female cat can have her first litter as young as six months, and she can have up to three litters each year, with an average five or six kittens per litter. It has been calculated that a single female and her descendants could produce 420,000 kittens in a mere seven years—quite an over-population problem.

Without supervision, a cat can be expecting another litter before her kittens are weaned.

Feline matriarchs

The most prolific mother recorded in feline history was Texan tabby Dusty, who lived in the 1950s and produced 420 documented kittens in her lifetime. Mother of the largest litter was a four-year-old Burmese called Tarawood Antigone, who in August 1970 produced 19 kittens—15 of which survived. And the oldest mother, Kitty from Staffordshire, bore her final two kittens (of a total of 218) when she was 30 years old.

Heroic mother

In April 1996, firefighters tackling a blaze at an abandoned building in Brooklyn were horrified to see a small cat dash into the flames. With a

AGE	DEVELOPMENT
0–3 weeks	Sight, smell, and hearing develop; dawn of social awareness—kittens separated from mother and siblings at this stage may never develop normal social skills.
4 weeks	Senses of smell and hearing well developed; interaction with littermates; walking; teeth erupting.
5 weeks	Sight fully mature; fully mobile, able to avoid obstacles, right themselves, stalk, pounce; acquiring grooming skills.
7 weeks	Developing motor abilities, social skills, and adult sleeping patterns.
7–14 weeks	Most active play period—learning social and practical skills by play; starting weaning.
3–6 months	Development of social ranking. Kittens weaned and less dependent on mother.
6–12 months	Adolescence; exploring social rank and challenging for position; beginnings of sexual maturity.

A battered Scarlett receives the blessing of the church from the Reverend Maier. Her heroism in saving her kittens brought nationwide fame.

four-week-old litter trapped inside, Scarlett ignored her horrific burns and made five trips into the fire to retrieve her five kittens. In a spate of publicity, the former stray was nursed back to health in an animal shelter before being adopted by a proud new owner.

Paternity puzzles

A female cat can mate with, and conceive by, more than one male when she is in heat, meaning that kittens born in the same litter may well have different fathers. As many as one in four pregnant cats may be carrying kittens sired by more than one mate. It's a survival technique to make use of the widest range of genes available—and an explanation why litters may include a variety of colors and sizes.

Cloned kitties

In 2002, scientists in Texas produced the first cloned cat, a calico called CopyCat, or CC for short. Although an exact genetic copy of her "parent," CC looks quite different because the calico pattern depends on where pigment develops in the embryo. Subsequently a Californian cloning company displayed a pair of cloned Bengals and offered their services to wealthy pet owners hoping to replicate their cats.

Cloned kittens Tabouli and Baba Ganoush were created in Texas in 2004.

Foster mothers

Cats with kittens are often so full of mother love that they are ready to adopt orphans of other species, including what would normally be prey animals ranging from sparrows to rats. One of the most unusual adoptions occurred at Twyford Wildlife Centre, Evesham, England, when a cat called Chief fostered a baby eagle owl along with her kittens.

THE CAT WHO WALKS BY HIMSELF?

Not so antisocial

Cats are usually seen as independent, solitary creatures. Most small wildcats do indeed fit the solitary stereotype, but it is now accepted that domestic cats don't. They don't form packs like dogs with a distinct social hierarchy, but they do enjoy a rich and complex social life. It seems that over centuries of living with humans, selective breeding for friendliness has developed sociability among cats.

Cats have more family feeling than is often recognized. Littermates usually remain pals for life and appreciate each other's company.

Two cats are often better than one. As well as being company for each other, they benefit from mental stimulation and exercise through play.

Feline friendships

Cats living in groups or large colonies hang out with family and friends. Researchers looking for a formal social structure based on dominance ranking with "top cats" and "underlings" were surprised to find that what counts in cat society is kinship, with family ties often enduring into adult life, and simple personal friendships between unrelated cats.

Cats like company

Cats who are left alone can become lonely and bored, and may develop destructive habits to pass the time. Human company is great, but another cat provides society, entertainment, and exercise even when an owner goes out. Adopting two kittens at the same time is easiest: adults take time to make friends (if they do so at all), and cats that are used to living alone often refuse to accept an intruder.

... but not crowds

Too many cats crowded together in a limited space will suffer from stress. Lack of personal space turns confident cats into aggressive bullies, forces timid cats to hide away, and produces behavioral problems like excessive urine marking. How many is too many depends on individuals and circumstances. Cats that are used to being solitary may find one other cat in the home one too many.

Bear with me

Cats often form close friendships with other species in the same household, usually dogs, but some have more unusual friends. At an Oregon wildlife refuge, a cat and a grizzly bear are inseparable companions, and at Berlin Zoo

Muschi and the black bear are inseparable friends who share a cage at Berlin Zoo.

a cat called Muschi adopted a black bear. When the bear was shut away during cage alteration work, the distraught cat sat outside the cage pining until at last she was allowed back in with her friend.

Sociability

Like people, some cats are more sociable than others. Much depends on social experience during kittenhood: cats that didn't mix with other cats when young are generally less enthusiastic about company as adults. Heredity also plays a part: friendly parents tend to produce friendly offspring, and the father's temperament seems to be particularly influential.

Introductions

The best way to introduce a new cat to a resident cat is to start with indirect encounters by nose. Keep the cats apart at first, letting them become familiar with each other's scent first by swapping sleeping blankets between them and letting them take turns in different rooms. When they meet face-to-face, it will not be as complete strangers, as they will already share a degree of "family smell."

Learning social skills

The key period when kittens acquire social habits is between the ages of 2 and 12 weeks—at an earlier age than puppies. This is when they learn to cope with and enjoy the company of other cats—and any other species to which they are exposed. Orphan kittens that are bottle reared may never learn to "talk cat," and kittens need handling during the socialization period to grow up people friendly.

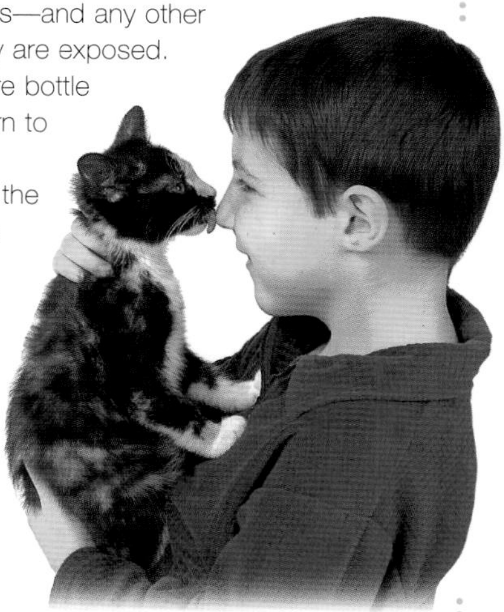

Kittens who are cuddled and played with grow up to be friendly; kittens who are ignored tend to remain shy.

HUNTERS

Natural-born mousers

Cats are designed to hunt small prey, and the natural world is their shopping mall. Scientists

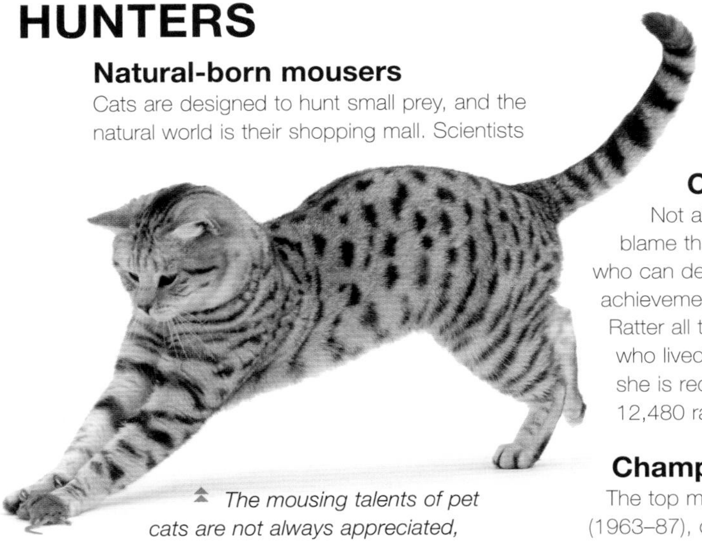

The mousing talents of pet cats are not always appreciated, especially when Puss brings his prize indoors!

calculate that domestic cats hunt and eat a range of about a thousand different species—compared with big cats, which may be restricted to fewer than a hundred. Above all, they are rodent specialists. Studies indicate that 60–70 percent of a cat's prey consists of small mammals, 20–30 percent birds, and 10 percent other animals.

Lethal lessons

Some pet cats hunt; some don't. It all depends on what their mothers taught them. Kittens born to mothers who are good hunters grow up to be hunters themselves, but nonhunting mothers produce nonhunting offspring. The moves for hunting come naturally, but kittens will use them only in play unless their mother shows them the practical application.

Champion ratter

Not all cats will tackle rats, and who can blame them? Rats are formidable opponents who can deliver a nasty bite. This makes the achievement of the feline World Champion Ratter all the more impressive. A female tabby who lived at London's White City Stadium, she is recorded to have caught a staggering 12,480 rats over a six-year period.

Champion mouser

The top mouser on record was Towser (1963–87), official pest-control officer at Glenturret Distillery, Scotland. During her long career she caught a total of 28,899 mice, as well as an uncounted number of rats, rabbits, and pheasants. Her tally earned her the title of

World champion mouser Towser (left) is commemorated by a statue and plaque (right) in her hunting grounds at Glenturret.

World Mouse-catching Champion, and in 1997 she was commemorated by a statue in the distillery grounds.

Cats won Agincourt!

Legend claims that cats won the Battle of Agincourt for the English in 1415. It is said that the English took their cats with them to guard their stores from rats and mice, but their French opponents didn't. As a result, the bowstrings of the French archers were nibbled by rats, whereas those of the English survived undamaged—so that's why the English won!

Tom and Jerry

Perhaps the most famous, if least successful, of mousers is Tom of the animated cartoon series *Tom and Jerry*. The series revolves around Tom's fruitless attempts to catch the much brighter mouse, Jerry. Starting in 1941 with *The Midnight Snack*, the series extended to more than 150 short movies, winning Tom and Jerry more Oscars than any other cartoon characters in Hollywood history.

This illustration from a medieval bestiary depicts cats in their valued role as mousers.

Wildlife destroyers

The cat's hunting prowess worries many conservationists. A 2001 report estimated that British cats kill some 275 million prey animals a year, and a study in Wisconsin concluded that the state's cats killed 20 to 150 million songbirds annually. Some argue that flawed statistics make the cat a scapegoat, but across the world laws are being brought in to protect local wildlife.

The better mousetrap

According to Ralph Waldo Emerson, "If a man can ... make a better mouse-trap than his neighbor ... the world will make a beaten path to his door." As the best mousetraps ever, cats have been exported worldwide for rodent control. Though this has often created a new problem as feral cats have multiplied, in 2004 Mexican authorities sought to import 700 cats to Chihuahua to deal with a major rat infestation.

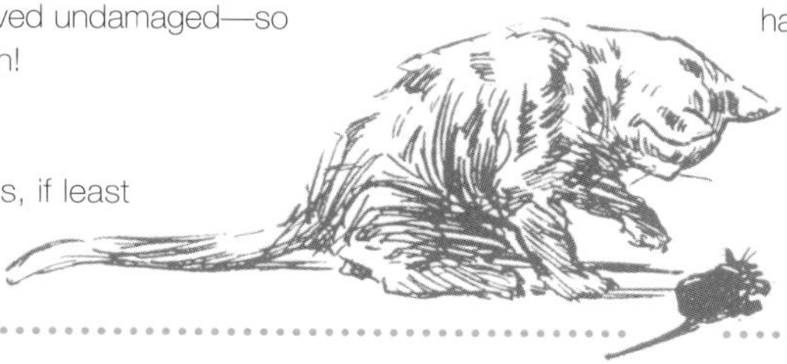

LET SLEEPING CATS LIE

Sleepyheads

Domestic cats spend more time asleep than any other mammals: most cats sleep for some two-thirds of their lives, and kittens and "senior citizens" spend up to 80 percent of their time asleep. Unlike us, cats don't divide their days into one sleep session and one waking session, but alternate short spells of sleep and waking throughout the day and night.

Cats like to choose their own beds. Some will accept the bed we have bought for them, but many adopt less obviously appealing sites.

Why do cats sleep so much?

In the wild, predators alternate short bursts of energetic hunting with long stretches of rest to build up energy reserves. Domestic cats follow the same pattern even when dinner arrives in their bowl upon demand with no effort on their part. If there is nothing interesting to do, they sleep. Bored indoor cats who lack company and stimulus sleep even more, "turning off" while their owners are out.

A dozing cat looks completely relaxed, but most of the time he is still fully on the alert.

Catnapping

About three-quarters of a cat's sleeping time is spent "on standby" in a very light sleep from which she can waken instantly ready for action. Cats are so good at this that we call a refreshing light doze a cat nap. These naps last about 10–30 minutes at a time, during which the muscles are never completely relaxed and the cat's ears and nose are still on full alert.

Flat cats and others

You can tell what kind of sleep your cat is enjoying from its position. Cat naps are often taken in a crouching position, with paws tucked underneath and head upright—relaxed but ready for action. For deep sleep cats favor curling into a snug ball, with nose, paws, and tail tucked tightly in. Confident cats sometimes sleep sprawled flat out on their sides like dogs, taking up lots of territory.

Do cats dream?

Cats spend short periods (up to ten minutes at a time) in deep sleep, when the body is completely relaxed and the "alarm system" turned off. During deep sleep, the brain is active, the eyes move rapidly behind closed lids, and paws and whiskers may twitch. In humans, REM (rapid eye movement) sleep is when we dream. Presumably it is the same for cats, though we can only guess what they dream about.

Sleeping partners

Most cats are quite happy sleeping alone, but cats that live together often sleep together, sharing warmth and the comfort of the "family smell." For the same reason, cats like to share their owners' beds, and if they are friendly with the family dog, it will be adopted as a mattress. Close physical contact with family, feline or otherwise, makes a cat feel secure, especially at bedtime.

Feline friends often sleep together, often endearingly clasped in each other's arms, for the sake of comfort and security.

Ideal bed

A popular poem by Eleanor Farjeon (1881–1965) claims, "Cats sleep anywhere." Their choice of bed may sometimes seem odd to us, but they do have certain criteria when choosing a sleeping place. They look for safety (enclosed spaces such as cupboards are favorites), the right temperature (shade in summer, near a heater in winter), and also somewhere that smells like home—owners' beds being popular for that reason.

Many cats like to sleep in high places, where they feel secure. In the wild this helps to keep them safe from predators.

TERRITORIAL AFFAIRS

Time-shares

In urban areas, as many as ten cats may share overlapping territories. They keep the peace by following a fairly regular timetable so they can usually avoid unexpected encounters, and by recognizing communal pathways where a neighbor can cross the territory unchallenged. The "top cat" in the area picks "prime times," such as when a favorite seat catches the morning sun, and the rest fit their time slots around him.

How big is a territory?

Territory size depends on food availability: where food is plentiful, a smaller area suffices. Males generally have larger ranges than females. Various studies have shown male ferals ranging over two square miles (5 sq km), farm cats with areas up to 50 acres (under a tenth of a square mile) (20 ha), and suburban cats averaging 17 acres (7 ha). Indoor cats can be content with very small territories, provided their basic needs are met, although over-crowding is likely to cause stress.

Both male and female cats carry out urine marking, although the habit is commonest (and most pungent) in un-neutered males.

Territory marking

Cats mark their territory with visual and smell signals, scratching marking posts or rubbing themselves against them to leave scent, spraying urine and depositing feces. These signals are not simple "Keep Out" signs for other cats, but bulletin boards where daily notices are posted to be read, informing feline neighbors who has been where and when, along with more detailed information.

Indoor cats

Where several cats are confined indoors, most of the house is usually held as common territory, but individuals will own, or at least have a time-share in, certain favored spots. Territorial rules help a cat to feel secure: if the cats in a

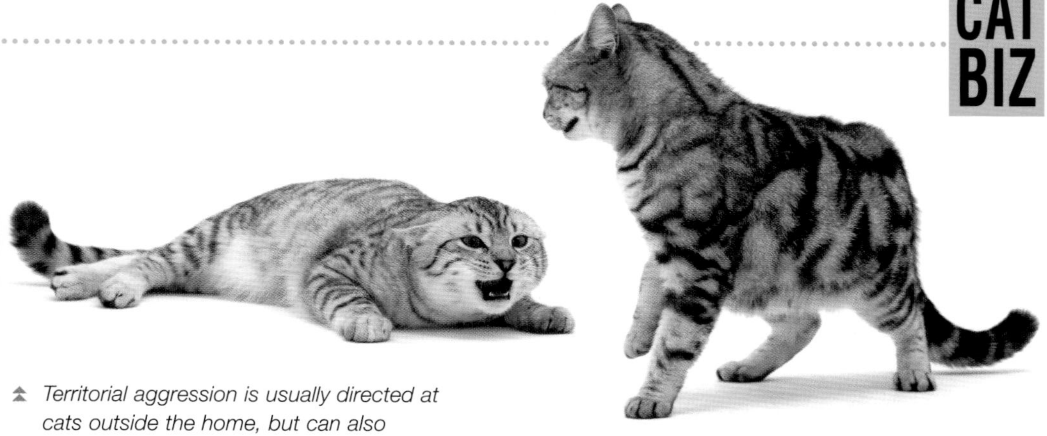

Territorial aggression is usually directed at cats outside the home, but can also become a problem between housemates.

household don't get along, or are overcrowded, they will feel driven to lay down the rules more emphatically by increasing scent marking—not an acceptable language to their owners.

Territorial defense

Cats naturally defend their territory against intruders, using threats or real violence. Territorial aggression may be a problem when a new cat is adopted into the home, when a kitten grows up to compete with an older cat for territory, or when neighboring cats trespass. In multicat households, quite often a cat who gets along well with most of the others may object to one individual who simply rubs him the wrong way.

Smelly problems

Both male and female cats urine-mark territory by spraying on vertical surfaces as well as squatting. If they urine-mark indoors, the message intended for other cats is pungent enough to trouble the noses of human cohabitees. If medical causes can be ruled out, this habit is usually caused by stress, but for some cats just seeing other animals outside can be enough to prompt marking behavior.

Moving to a new home

For a cat, moving to a new home is particularly traumatic because it means the loss of a known territory. To acclimatize your pet to a new home, you may need to keep him shut in for two or three weeks while the house acquires his familiar scent, perhaps taking him out on a harness and lead to explore the new outdoors area. Some cats settle in faster than others, but most need a gradual introduction to their new territory.

Accustom your cat to his traveling carrier before any move to help him feel safe inside it.

CATS AND WATER

Water bowls should be rinsed out and refilled twice a day.

Some like it wet

Cats proverbially hate water, but do they really? Most hate being forcibly bathed and many dislike going out in the rain; but some like playing with water, some even enjoy swimming, and of course all cats need to drink. They drink less than dogs, as their bodies conserve water better, but they must have access to drinking water at all times—especially cats on a dry-food diet who can't obtain water from their food.

The swimming breed

One breed, the Turkish Van, is famous for its love of water and delight in swimming—in fact they are nicknamed "swimming cats." The breed evolved on the shores of Turkey's Lake Van, where visitors were amazed to see them fishing and playing in the shallows. Van cats are individuals and not all of them are water babies, but many will happily jump into water and even join their owners in the shower.

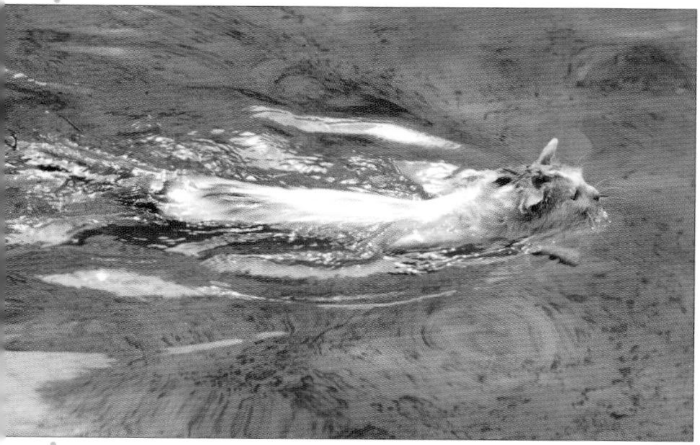

Legend says that Van cats originated with a pair who swam impatiently ashore from the Ark.

Reluctant sea cats

In 2004, Nemo, a ten-week-old ginger kitten, was rescued from the Gulf of Mexico after he was spotted swimming for his life three miles from land, presumably having fallen from a boat. In the same year tabby kitten Gollum fell off her catamaran home near the Seychelles Islands and was presumed eaten by sharks, but a few days later swam triumphantly back to the boat, wet but unharmed.

Bothersome baths

Cats rarely need bathing, and even more rarely cooperate in the process—sometimes described as a martial art! If a bath is essential, it's easier with two people, one to hold and one to wash. Fill the container to about half the cat's height and check the water temperature before inserting the cat, then shampoo gently from the neck downward. Thorough rinsing is essential: soap left on the skin will cause irritation.

Fussy drinkers

Cats have strong views on what they should drink. Some spurn a nice clean water bowl in favor of a muddy puddle, a dripping tap, or even the toilet. This is generally because cats assess water on its smell. To a cat's nose, drinking water may reek of unacceptable chemicals, or bowls may carry the taint of detergent or stale food. To minimize problems, avoid plastic bowls (which retain odors) and change water twice daily.

Gone fishing

Proverbially, "the cat would have fish but would not wet her feet." Though some wildcats regularly go fishing, most domestic cats are not prepared to brave the water in order to catch fish. However, as owners of goldfish ponds know, brightly colored fish moving about in a small space can prove too tempting to resist, and some cats become quite skilled at flicking fish out of the water with a paw.

▲ *A fish in a bowl is just too tempting to be ignored. To keep both cats and fish as pets, it is safest to have an aquarium with a lid.*

Using the tongue as a ladle makes drinking from a tap easy. Many cats find running water more attractive than their own water bowls.

Built-in spoon

Cats drink by ladling water into their mouths, using their tongues as spoons. The tongue curls down and backward (the opposite way to human tongues) to form a spoon-shaped hollow in which to carry water to the mouth. A cat fills its mouth with three or four "spoonfuls" before swallowing. Members of the cat and dog families are the only species that lap water in this fashion.

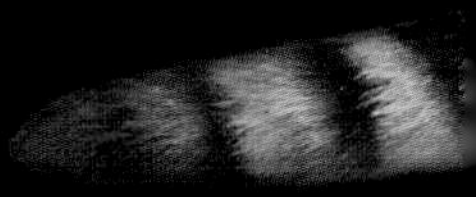

THE THINGS

CATS DO

CATS IN WAR

Feline shields

Legend says that cats helped King Cambyses of Persia to conquer Egypt in 535 B.C. Knowing the Egyptians' reverence for cats as sacred animals, the Persian soldiers attached cats to their shields. Hampered by their concerns not to injure any cat, the Egyptians lost the day, and Cambyses was able to take over the country and start his own dynasty.

Clearly no animal lover, Cambyses II follows up his military abuse of Egypt's cats by slaying the sacred Apis bull of Memphis.

Chemical warfare

In the 16th century German artillery officer Christopher of Hapsburg came up with a plan to use cats as gas bombs. The cats, he proposed, would have jars of poison gas attached to their backs (with the openings facing backward) and be driven among enemy troops to spread alarm and poisonous fumes. His plan was presented to the Council of One and Twenty in Strasbourg, but was never put into use.

Patriotic ratters

In World War I, the British army employed 500,000 cats as gas detectors and ratters in the trenches. As guardians of food stores they were so important to the war effort that World War II saw thousands of cats donated by the British public and also by the U.S. via a Cats For Europe scheme, with an official powdered milk ration for "all cats engaged in work of national importance."

Messenger cat

Russian cat Mourka won his place in history during the siege of Stalingrad in 1942, braving heavy sniper fire to carry messages between companies about enemy gun emplacements. As far as he was concerned, he was merely visiting the company kitchens, but his contribution was invaluable. As the *London Times*

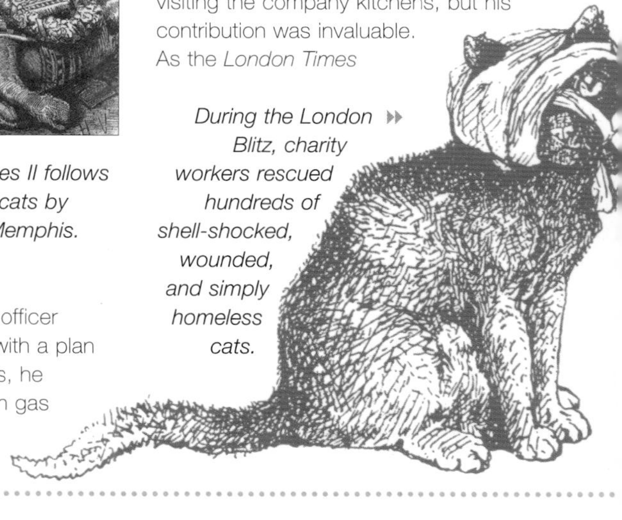

During the London Blitz, charity workers rescued hundreds of shell-shocked, wounded, and simply homeless cats.

Two victims of war: a Russian girl and her cat wander through the rubble of their home after the departure of the Germans, c.1944.

reported, "he has shown himself worthy of Stalingrad, and whether for cat or man there can be no higher praise."

Churchill's aide

Sir Winston Churchill was addicted to cats, and during World War II his black cat Nelson not only attended War Cabinet meetings but had his own chair reserved for him in the Cabinet Room. Churchill pointed out that Nelson also assisted the war effort by acting as his personal hot water bottle, thus saving on fuel.

Dambuster's cat

Commander Guy Gibson, the famous dambuster bomber pilot of World War II, often took his cat Windy with him on his missions. Gibson's famous black Labrador Nigger was featured in the 1954 film *The Dambusters*, but Windy was somehow forgotten, despite his status as "an all-swimming and all-flying cat [who] put in more flying hours than most cats."

Morale boosters

Soldiers have always felt better for adopting mascots, and many cat mascots have earned their keep as "stress busters." One American infantry battalion returning home from the war in Iraq went to huge efforts to ensure that their feline mascot, Hammer, returned with them "because we consider him one of our troops," and in April 2004 Hammer arrived in San Francisco to start a new life as an American citizen.

Mustard, mascot of a World War I tank, poses for his photograph with his owner, American serviceman Sergeant Paul Preston.

SHIPS' CATS

Sailors' superstitions

Since ancient times, ships have carried cats to deal with mice and rats aboard. The belief that having a cat aboard brought good luck is also an ancient one. Sailors believed that cats could predict and even influence the weather: it was said that cats carried a magic wind in their tails, and could raise a storm if ill treated. Throwing a cat overboard brought terrible bad luck on the ship.

The Dickin Medal was instituted in 1943 by Maria Dickin to honor the work of animals in war. To date some 60 animals have been awarded the "Animals' VC." Simon is the only cat to receive this award.

Whiskey, mascot of HMS Duke of York *in World War II, slept calmly through the battle when the German battle cruiser* Scharnhorst *was sunk.*

So famous that a cat officer was appointed to deal with his mail, Simon was a reluctant celebrity who often hid from photographers.

War hero

Simon, mascot of HMS *Amethyst*, was the only cat to be awarded the Dickin Medal (the "Animals' VC"). Born in Hong Kong, where he was adopted by the ship's crew, he was aboard in 1948 when the *Amethyst* was besieged by Communist batteries in the Yangtse River for two months. Despite being wounded, Simon carried on with his duties of ratting and keeping up the crew's spirits until the *Amethyst* made its escape.

Circumnavigator

Explorer Matthew Flinders, who mapped the coast of Australia in 1802, was accompanied by his black and white cat Trim. Together they circumnavigated the world, as well as sailing three times around Australia. During their voyages, Trim learned to catch a rope and even to swim. He took a great interest in watching the officers at their navigation, so much so that Flinders insisted the cat was keen on nautical astronomy.

Rescue at sea

Sixteenth-century geographer Richard Hakluyt recorded sailors' care for their cats. On one of his voyages, the ship's cat jumped overboard. The ship had already lost time waiting for a wind, but as soon as the cat was spotted struggling in the water almost half a mile away, the master sent half a dozen men in a skiff to her rescue. "I hardly believe," Hakluyt remarked, "they would have made such haste … if one of the company had bene in the like perill."

Antarctic endurance

Ship's carpenter Henry McNeish took his tabby cat Mrs. Chippy on Ernest Shackleton's 1914–16 Trans-Antarctic Expedition. Ratting, teasing the sled dogs, even surviving a fall overboard, Mrs. Chippy was a valued team member; but when the *Endurance* was abandoned, trapped in pack ice, all animals were shot. McNeish never forgot his cat, or forgave Shackleton. In 2004, a life-size bronze statue of Mrs. Chippy was placed on McNeish's grave.

Mrs. Chippy's statue now reclines on Henry McNeish's grave in belated recognition of her contribution to the Trans-Antarctic Expedition.

Stowaway star

A New Zealand feline known only as Colin's Cat made headlines in 2001 when she accidentally stowed away aboard methanol tanker *Tomiwaka,* bound for Korea. Her plight aroused national interest, and when she was finally flown home from Korea, she was made honorary ambassador for her home city of New Plymouth "in recognition of her involvement in the enhancement of international relations."

Tanker terminal officer Gordon MacPherson, who brought Colin's Cat home, with his protégé. Today an older and wiser cat sticks to the wharf and no longer boards vessels.

Unluckiest—or luckiest?

In 1941, ship's cat Oscar had three ships sunk under him and lived to tell the tale. Found swimming among the wreckage of German battleship *Bismarck*, Oscar was adopted by British destroyer HMS *Cossack*—and when that sank, by the aircraft carrier *Ark Royal*. When a German submarine sank *Ark Royal*, Oscar escaped again—but enough was enough, and he retired ashore to the sailors' home at Belfast.

TRAVELING CATS

Astrocat

In 1963, a French cat called Felix became the first feline astronaut. French scientists had 14 cats in training for space flight, ten of whom disqualified themselves by overeating. A black-and-white stray from Paris, Felix was launched into space from the Sahara Desert, hurtling 130 miles (210 km) skyward before her capsule was released from the rocket to parachute down to a safe landing.

The flight of Felix, first cat in space, was celebrated by this Comoros Republic stamp.

Trans-Atlantic pioneer

Kiddo, a gray tabby cat, accompanied the airship *America* on its unsuccessful 1910 attempt at a trans-Atlantic crossing, but after three days cat and crew had to be rescued by a steamship. However, tabby kitten Whoopsy (later renamed Jazz by American admirers) outdid him in 1919 when he stowed away aboard British airship R-34 to complete the first trans-Atlantic crossing from Britain to America.

America*'s attempt to fly across the Atlantic failed after 1,000 miles (1,600 km). Among the crew rescued by steamer was the cat Kiddo.*

Antarctic explorer

Nigger, ship's cat on Captain Scott's expedition to the South Pole (1910–13), was the first cat to land and overwinter in the Antarctic. His comfort was not neglected: he had his own hammock aboard ship, with his personal blanket and pillow, faring better than Nansen, ship's cat on the 1897 Belgian Antarctic Expedition, who succumbed to the cruel conditions.

Roof rider

In 2005, C. B., an orange tabby from Idaho, fancied a car ride with her owner. When she was firmly removed from the backseat, she hopped on to the roof rack. Owner Torri Hutchinson drove ten miles before another driver flagged her down and pointed out her unsuspected passenger, hanging on for dear life. C. B. was duly retrieved, but apparently showed no further interest in car travel.

Long-distance flights

Another cat called Felix escaped from his crate on a Pan Am jet and hid in the cargo hold,

Californian stowaway Felix (seen here in quarantine) racked up an impressive number of air miles aboard a Pan Am jet in 1988.

where he flew nearly 180,000 miles (290,000 km)—equal to seven times around the world—before he was recaptured at London and flown home at last to Los Angeles. He was outdone by Hamlet, who also became lost aboard a plane and was trapped behind a panel where he remained undiscovered for six weeks, traveling nearly 600,000 miles (1 million km).

Under his own steam

In 1939 ship's cat Sidney James pulled off an astonishing feat when he was accidentally left behind at Bootle, near Liverpool. The ship's crew was upset at their loss—and amazed when they arrived at Buenos Aires to find him waiting for them. Finding himself abandoned, Sidney had boarded a fast mail boat also headed to Buenos Aires, which left later the same night to arrive six days earlier.

An uncomfortable seat

Cats' love of heat sometimes leads them to slip under car hoods to enjoy the warmth of the engine, where they may not be noticed in time. A cat called Buttons made this mistake in 1983 and set a record for the greatest distance traveled by any cat under the hood of a car: an uncomfortable six-hour journey of 300 miles (480 km). Astonishingly, she was unharmed—and was flown home courtesy of a compassionate airline.

Touring Britain

When writer Frederick Harrison decided to spend seven months exploring Britain in a camper van, his traveling companion was Pugwash, a thoroughly adaptable cat who took life on the road in his stride. A friendly, laid-back character who leaned against walls to sniff flowers, the town-bred Pugwash enjoyed investigating the countryside on his own at night, returning to the van with a collection of mice as holiday souvenirs.

In 1996 Norfolk cat Muffin hid from dogs in the engine bay of this car. He was discovered unharmed 140 miles (225 km) later.

INCREDIBLE JOURNEYS

Magnetic navigation

Cats' ability to find their way home seems to depend on navigating by the Earth's magnetic field. Researchers found that cats placed in an enclosed maze with exits at the different points of the compass generally picked the exits that faced directly homeward. But when the scientists tied powerful magnets to the cats' collars, it disrupted their biological compasses and they could no longer tell which exit to choose.

The Earth's magnetic field may be only part of a cat's navigation system: the angle of the sun and its own biological clock may play a part.

Longest journey

In 1952 the Wood family moved from California to Oklahoma, leaving their Persian cat Sugar with a neighbor to spare her the journey. Two weeks later Sugar disappeared—to appear 14 months later at the Woods' new home. She was clearly identifiable by a hip deformity—yet despite this she had traveled 1,500 miles (2,400 km) over desert and mountains, to a place she had never before visited, to be reunited with her family.

No place like home

Some cats have made marathon journeys to find their way home. A German cat called Minosch walked 1,500 miles (2,400 km) home after being lost on vacation in Turkey in 1981. An Australian cat called Silky was lost 1,472 miles (2,370 km) from home but made it back on her own; and an American tomcat called Ninja, whose owners moved from Utah to Washington State in 1996, didn't think much of the move and headed the 850 miles (1,370 km) back home to arrive a year later.

Better late than never

In 1982, Barbara Paule of Pennsylvania lost her cat Muddy Water White while driving through Ohio, 450 miles (725 km) from home. Three years later he arrived, tired and thin, on his home doorstep. His distinctive markings (a black coat sprinkled with white, and a very leathery lower lip) enabled the local vet to confirm his identity.

Best seller

Real-life journeys like these inspired Sheila Burnford to write her best-selling novel *The Incredible Journey* (1961) in which two dogs and a Siamese cat travel 250 miles (400 km) through the Canadian wilderness to find their family. The much-loved book inspired three films, *The Incredible Journey* (1963), *Homeward Bound: The Incredible Journey* (1992), and *Homeward Bound II: Lost in San Francisco* (1996).

In the three films based on The Incredible Journey, *Tao the Siamese becomes Sassy the Himalayan, seen here confidently leading her canine companions.*

Determined cats

When the owners of a middle-aged English cat called Pilsbury moved a mere 8 miles (13 km) to their new home, they didn't expect to find themselves making regular return journeys. However, Pilsbury had to be retrieved from his old home 40 times, making the trip at least once a week. Even more determined was Tigger, who returned to his old home more than 75 times—only a three-mile trip, but a long walk for a cat with only three legs.

Rusty's travels

A ginger tom called Rusty achieved a similar feat—but faster. In 1949 his owner moved from Boston, Massachusetts, to Chicago, Illinois, but decided not to take Rusty. The cat had other ideas and followed him. It took him 83 days to complete the 950-mile (1,530-km) journey.

Tracking a train

A kitten called Pitchon was determined not to lose her owner. When Fernand Schmitt joined the French army, he left Pitchon behind with a neighbor. Eleven days later, Pitchon joined him at the army barracks in Strasbourg, 75 miles (120 km) from home. She had apparently followed his train, for Schmitt was able to find witnesses who had seen the kitten trekking along the railway tracks and her arrival at Strasbourg.

In 2005 Wisconsin cat Emily hid in a cargo container that ended up on board a ship bound for France. Identified by her collar tag, she was flown home business class!

CATS WITH JOBS

Post Office cats

Cats were first officially appointed as British Post Office employees in 1868, at a wage of a shilling a week. Prime Minister Ramsay MacDonald ascribed his success in life to a black cat in a London post office that was trained to lick stamps: he employed its services to stamp an envelope containing an article he was sending to *The Times*. Its subsequent acceptance marked the start of his career.

Railway cats

Cats have also been employed by railways as pest controllers, although the most famous, Tiddles, who lived at London's Paddington Station for 13 years, was no mouser. Adopted by station staff in 1970 as a six-week-old kitten, Tiddles became a well-known character. In 1982, overfed by admirers who supplied him with delicacies from chicken livers to steak, he achieved the title of London Fat Cat Champion.

Tiddles of Paddington Station received fan mail from all over the world—and so many tidbits that he eventually weighed 32 lb. (14.5 kg).

Matilda of the Algonquin Hotel is a New York celebrity who holds an annual birthday party and has her own e-mail address.

Hotel cat

New York's Algonquin Hotel is almost as famous for its cats as for its accommodation. The first, Rusty, arrived in the early 1930s, rehomed from a Broadway stage show. He was renamed Hamlet, a name officially borne by each of his successors until recently. The current incumbent (and the first pedigree to hold the post), is a Ragdoll called Matilda, whose annual birthday party is one of the hotel's great social events.

Zoo cats

Many zoos have employed cats to control disease-spreading rodents. In 1938 New York Zoo employed four cats to patrol the aquarium area and keep down rats. There was a problem early on when one of the cats killed a valuable fish, but the ingenious head keeper tackled this by leaving some electric eels within the cats' reach. The trick worked: the cats never fancied fish again, but concentrated on ratting.

Library cats

Library cats have a long and noble tradition. At one time the St. Petersburg library employed 300 cats as mousers, and today the U.S. has a Library Cat Society to honor its feline workers. Recently Woodford Library (Connecticut) was the center of a heated campaign regarding its cat Fred, evicted for the sake of a cat-allergic trustee—which cost the library $80,000 when Fred-loving notables cut it out of their wills.

Hospital cat

For 16 years Mittens the black cat was a much-loved member of the staff at New Zealand's Taranaki Hospital. Mittens had the freedom of the wards and blotted his copybook only once, when he was accused of fishing in the children's aquarium. Valued as a morale booster for staff and patients alike, he even had his own bank account to cover his living expenses, funded by a fortnightly raffle.

A growing number of therapy cats are now approved hospital visitors, but Mittens was unusual in being a permanent hospital resident.

Cats and books often go together well—many libraries employ cats as mousers.

Political cat

Humphrey, a fluffy black-and-white stray, became one of Britain's feline stars after he moved into the prime minister's London residence at 10 Downing Street during Margaret Thatcher's incumbency. He was one of the few occupants to outlast her, remaining throughout John Major's term of office. After eight years as official Mouser to the Cabinet Office, he was retired to the country when Tony Blair moved in.

Museum cats

In 1908, Black Jack, resident cat at the British Museum, marched into the museum carrying a tiny kitten, which he presented to the keeper of Egyptian cat mummies. Tended by the museum staff cats, the kitten grew up to become Mike the Museum Cat, keeper of the main gate for 20 years and, in his own mind, controller of the local pigeons—although staff were always able to release his captures unharmed.

THEATER CATS

A long tradition

Since Elizabethan times, when stagehands were often retired sailors who brought the ship's cat with them, theaters have kept a resident cat as mascot and mouser. The modern world with its health and safety rules has put an end to the custom in most theaters—although Shakespeare's Globe in London, upholder of tradition, has not one but two cats, Jack and Cleo, who are as well known as many actors in the company.

Jack and Cleo (stage names Portia and Brutus) of the Globe Theatre achieved worldwide fame and even appeared on a Turkish TV show.

Theater superstitions

Cats in the theater have long been held to bring good luck—if they remain backstage. If they appear on stage during a performance, this is a bad omen (although many theater cats made a habit of this and were clearly exempt from this belief). Kicking a cat, quite rightly, is believed to bring bad luck. More oddly, some claim a cat's deposit in the dressing room to be a good omen—a notion perhaps designed to protect the offender from unwelcome retribution.

Minnie and mayhem

Black-and-white Minnie was one of New York's last great theater cats. Her sister was expelled for clawing up costumes, but Minnie was usually well behaved—apart from a famous foray on stage when Bobby Clark's act as a comic tortilla maker involved fresh dough, which she loved. Unaware of the cat behind him snatching at his props, Clark was baffled when the audience laughed in the wrong places.

Impromptu tiger

In 1951, the Palace Theatre in Redditch put on a performance of *White Cargo*, set in Africa. On the opening night, the theater cat strolled on stage to join co-stars Jon Holliday and Geoffrey Kendall. Unable to ignore him as he headed for center stage to peer over the footlights at the audience, Kendall came up with an inspired ad lib that brought the house down as he commanded, "Get that tiger out of here."

Gus the Theatre Cat

T. S. Eliot celebrated the role of theatrical felines in his creation of Gus, the Theatre Cat in his *Old Possum's Book of Practical Cats*. Gus is an old-stager recounting his past stage triumphs when he played "every possible part" and lamenting the decline of the modern theater. In the musical *Cats* Sir John Mills's touching performance as Gus was highly acclaimed.

Troublesome twins

Girl Cat and Boy Cat of London's Albery Theatre, acquired as mousers, have become well-known cast members. Boy Cat once interrupted *Pygmalion* to cross the stage and join the audience in a front-row seat, and during *Five Guys Named Moe* both cats hid under the stage, to erupt into the auditorium when the tap dancing began over their heads. Boy Cat also achieved fame by eating Princess Margaret's bouquet at a gala evening.

Ambrose the actor

From 1974 to 1985 London's Theatre Royal was the home of Ambrose, a smart black cat with a white shirt front whose frequent impromptu stage appearances gave both him and audiences much pleasure. Although some actors objected to being upstaged by a cat, the backstage crew were united in his defense. After his death, he was considered irreplaceable.

Old-timer

London's longest serving theater cat was Beerbohm, a handsome tabby who ruled the Globe (now the Gielgud) for 20 years and whose portrait may still be seen there. Audiences loved his occasional forays on stage, though upstaged actors were sometimes less thrilled. In old age, Beerbohm retired to Kent, where he died in 1995—the only cat ever to receive a front-page obituary in *The Stage* newspaper.

Beerbohm's portrait is proudly displayed at the Gielgud Theatre, formerly the Globe.

CHURCH CATS

Papal cats

Micetto, a red-and-gray cat, was born in the Vatican and became famous as the inseparable companion of the elderly Pope Leo XII (1760–1829), peeping out of the pope's white robes during papal audiences. However, the cat-loving pope of today, Benedict XVI, has to abide by a rule banning pets from Vatican apartments, and his beloved black-and-white Chico remains at his private residence in Tübingen, Germany.

Patron saint

St. Gertrude of Nivelles, a French abbess in the seventh century, is patron saint of cats. Her association with felines seems to have arisen from taking iconography literally. In art, she was depicted with mice, representing the souls in purgatory to whom she was devoted. This led to a folk belief that she could assist with rodent problems—which in turn linked her to that great mouser, the cat.

Although she had no known feline associations in life, St. Gertrude is now firmly established as patron saint of cats—as well as herbalists and travelers.

Not so saintly

Biggles, born in a mining village, took up a career in the church to become resident ratter at London's Westminster Abbey. A cat of great character, he amuses himself by lying in wait within a dense Virginia creeper, to leap out at passing dogs and tourists. He has also been known to sharpen his claws on the high altar, and received an official police warning after mauling a constable's trousers.

Tiddles, church cat at the Church of St. Mary the Virgin, Fairford, Gloucestershire, is affectionately remembered with a memorial stone outside the church he loved.

Cats of the monastery

France's blue cat, the Chartreux, is said to have been developed by medieval monks at the Grande Chartreux monastery near Grenoble, who were presented by 13th-century crusaders with blue cats from Syria, from which they bred distinctively colored cats with especially quiet voices, so they would not disturb meditations. Sadly, there is no evidence to support this appealing legend.

Monastery of the cats

Cyprus's "Monastery of the Cats" was founded in A.D. 325 by St. Helena of the Cross, who is said to have imported two shiploads of cats to deal with an infestation of snakes. Thereafter the monks always maintained at least 100 cats. The monastery fell into disrepair in the 16th century, but was reestablished in modern times as a Greek Orthodox convent and is once again famous for its hundreds of resident cats.

Faith was the first cat to win decorations for courage during the hard times of World War II.

Ecumenical cat

Author George Borrow, traveling in Wales in 1854, had an argument with his landlady at Llangollen when he fed a miserable, starving black cat. The cat, she explained, had been left behind by a Church of England vicar—and was therefore persecuted by the locals, Dissenters to a man. The tale had a happy ending when an English family moved in and offered the cat an Anglican home.

Keeping faith

Faith was the much-loved church cat of St. Augustine's and St. Faith's, in London. During World War II, her heroism in saving her kitten during a heavy air raid touched people's hearts across the world. She was awarded two silver medals, and her picture and a testimony to "the bravest cat in the world" were displayed in the church. Today she lies buried in the churchyard that was her home.

Changeable relationship

The cat's relationship with the church has had its ups and downs. Although the early Christian church viewed cats with deep suspicion as pagan beasts and even supported the persecution of the species, there have always been some clerical cat lovers, and in later, kinder times most churches and cathedrals had (and often still have) their resident felines.

Church mice may be famous for poverty, but church cats generally do rather well. Many have become well-known local characters, appreciated by visitors as well as regular churchgoers.

NINE LIVES

Record fall

Cats are famous for surviving amazing falls. The record holder is Andy, the pet of Florida senator Ken Myer, who fell 200 ft. (60 m) from the 16th floor of an apartment building, and lived to tell the tale. Another cat, Pussycat, fell a mere 120 ft. (36.5 m) from an 11th-floor balcony in London, and walked away after making a perfect landing on all four paws—though he suffered some loss of appetite for a few days.

This lucky New York tabby survived a 20-story fall and is seen here above the drop, safe in the arms of the owner.

Electric perch

In August 2005, curiosity nearly killed a Nevada cat who climbed up to investigate a bird's nest on top of an electricity pole. Touching a relay switch sparked off a flash fire that hurled him 40 ft (12 m) to the ground. Fire-fighters called to the resulting blaze found what they thought was a dead cat, but after being revived with oxygen he proved to be only singed and was expected to make a full recovery.

Underwater survival

Dutch ship's cat Peter survived nearly eight days underwater when his vessel, the *Tjoba*, sank in the River Rhine in December 1964. Presumed dead, he surfaced when the boat was salvaged from the bottom, having managed to hold his head up in an air pocket all that time, while his body remained below the surface of the water. He was nursed back to health, but stayed ashore thereafter.

Falling overboard is a natural hazard for ships' cats, but they are excellent, if reluctant, swimmers, and often manage to save themselves without human aid.

Concrete tomb

In 1974, a kitten exploring a building site in Skopje, Yugoslavia, was hiding inside the wooden shaper for a new wall when workmen

Lost for 18 days after the eptember 11, 2001, World de Center attack, Precious the Himalayan survived by drinking rainwater.

oured in the concrete. Fifty-three hours later, the men removed the wooden planks to discover the kitten encased in the wall—and alive, his nose pressed to a crack in the wood that enabled him to breathe. After carefully chiseling him out, they were left with a perfect kitten-shaped mold in the wall.

Python problems

An Australian cat called Nick went for a stroll in the mountains near his home. On his return, his owner was stroking him when he found the fur around Nick's neck ringed with small, sharp white objects. Staff at Queensland Museum dentified them as the teeth of a carpet python with an estimated length of about 6.5 ft. (2 m)—easily big enough to eat a cat. Nick evidently came very close to becoming a snake's dinner.

Endurance tests

Cats have survived being trapped without food or water for astonishing periods, like Smokey, who was stuck in a vending machine for 37 days in 1990, or Bruno, trapped under floorboards for 45 days. Both recovered fully from their ordeals—as did the nameless cat found alive n a collapsed building a full 80 days after the Taiwan earthquake of 1999, claiming the award for the longest post-earthquake survival by a cat.

Exploded kitten

In 1991, during the Persian Gulf conflict, U.S. Army antiterrorist squads were on the lookout for terrorist bombs planted in American cities, so when a cardboard box was left outside a courthouse, they naturally blew it up. From the wreckage emerged a very frightened kitten, injured but alive. He was rescued by the local deputy sheriff, who adopted him and gave him the appropriate name of Thunderball.

Stuck in a statue

In Christchurch, New Zealand, a jubilee memorial statue of Queen Victoria was erected in 1903 to great acclaim. However, it had to be taken down again when plaintive mews led to the realization that there was a cat trapped inside the hollow figure. Having hoisted the statue down from its pedestal, officials found the cat reluctant to emerge, and had to lure him out with a smelly fish before they could reinstate the memorial.

Cats' incredible climbing skills often help them to escape danger but sometimes lead them into some very sticky situations from which they may need rescuing.

TALENTED CATS

Retrievers

Egyptian paintings depict cats accompanying their owners hunting, apparently acting as retrievers—but it is unlikely that such scenes should be taken literally. Retrieving does not come naturally to cats as it does to gundogs. However, some individual cats will play Fetch with toys, and Kitty of the Black Swan pub, Newcastle, was famous for assisting darts players by retrieving their darts from the board.

A wall painting from a tomb in Thebes (c.1400 B.C.) shows a cat acting as a retriever while its master hunts for birds.

Painting with paws

Although painting chimpanzees and elephants have become quite well known, cats are relative newcomers to the art world. Most cats don't like getting paint on their paws, but some individuals are quite happy to paddle in a paint pot and wipe their paws on the canvas provided. Art collectors are now paying high prices for feline artworks, and one painting by a ginger tom called Bootsie fetched £50,000.

Engineers' assistant

America's Grand Coulee Dam was completed only with the help of a passing stray cat. Engineers struggled in vain to feed a steel cable through a conduit, until they spotted the cat investigating the end of the channel. Tying a string to its tail, they encouraged it to explore. When the cat emerged at the other end, the engineers were able to use the string to pull the cable through.

Circus stars

Some people say cats can't be trained, but when Russian circus performer Yuri Kuklachev found an abandoned kitten in the park in 1976, he decided to train it as a circus performer. This was such a success that Kuklachev went on to found the Moscow Cats Theatre *(above)*, with 120 cats who walk tightropes, do paw-stands, jump on cue, and balance balls on their noses—all the training achieved by kindness.

Psychic healer

In the 1980s Rogan, a marmalade cat based in London, achieved worldwide fame as a psychic healer, offering relief from various ailments by the "laying on of paws" and even through fur combings sent by mail. He also provided absent healing by sitting on sufferers' letters in a "psychic trance." After his death in 1986, his owner, Mrs. Bailey, felt guided by his spirit to adopt another cat to carry on his work.

Counting cat

Cuty-Boy, a cat from Dubai, hit the headlines in 2001 when owner Hema Mohan Chadra reported his passion for number crunching. The cream Persian can add, subtract, divide, multiply, and find square roots, indicating the correct answer by selecting from numbers displayed on cards. A local math teacher tested him on algebra, geometry, Pythagoras, and square roots and reported a right answer every time.

Biker cat

Black cat Rastus and motorcyclist Max Corkill were renowned across New Zealand for their partnership. Rastus rode confidently on the bike's fuel tank, wearing a custom-made helmet, racing goggles, and red-spotted bandana, while his human companion sported a badge inscribed "Cat Chauffeur." After their deaths in 1998 in a road accident, a parade of more than 1,000 bikers followed the two hearses to the crematorium.

This 1875 engraving by Harrison Weir for The Animal World *shows five cats who were apparently taught to ring bells in sequence. Evidently in Victorian times some cats' talents even extended to campanology!*

Easy Rider, feline-style. Rastus is seen perched on top of the fuel tank of Max Corkill's 1952 vintage Sunbeam S-7.

WEIRD AND WONDERFUL CATS

Four-eared cats

Rarely, cats are born with an extra pair of ears. Some have other linked abnormalities; others are normal. In 2004, a German animal shelter sought a home for four-eared Lilly, reporting, "She is healthy and can hear perfectly well but only through the front pair." A Russian kitten born in 2004 had no apparent problem coping with seven ears. Its owners claimed it had particularly good hearing, especially when called for meals.

Gizmo from Lafayette, Louisiana, has a second pair of ear flaps inside his normal ears.

Cats with wings

Winged cats have been reported since the 1890s. The wings range in length from 6 in. (15 cm) (an Oxford specimen found in 1933) to 23 in. (58 cm) (a Swedish cat found in 1949). Despite claims that such cats actually fly, the "wings" are actually useless extensions caused by an inherited skin disorder (feline cutaneous asthenia), which makes the skin extremely elastic so that it forms winglike folds.

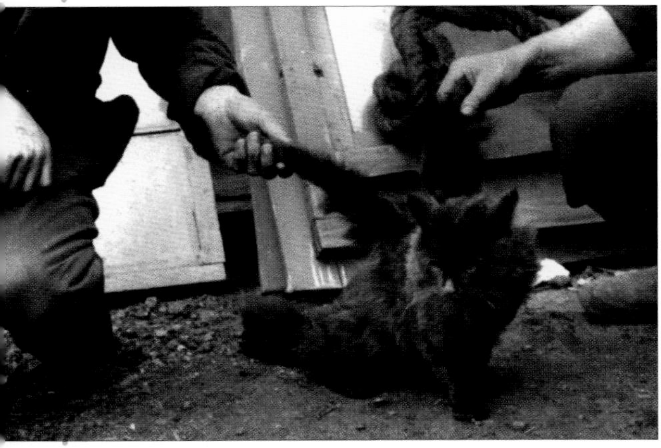

This winged cat made his home in a builder's yard in Manchester in the 1960s. His "wings" measured 11 in. (28 cm) from the shoulder blade.

Winged TV star

Winged cat Thomas, found in West Virginia in 1959, became a celebrity when he appeared on television, and again when there were legal proceedings over his ownership. However, when Thomas shed his wings a few months later, they turned out to be just long pads of matted fur. This is not an uncommon occurrence in neglected longhairs, and proved to be also the case with the winged cat from Ontario, Canada, shot in 1966.

Cactus cat

A bizarre beast with prickly hair, forked tail, and sharp blades on its forelegs, the Cactus Cat was part of the folklore of the American Wild West. Its terrible nocturnal screeches were caused by intoxication after drinking the

ended with the cats hurling themselves into the sea. Their fears were well founded. After the "disease of the dancing cats" had spread to humans, it was identified as mercury poisoning, caused by pollution from a local factory—but too late to save its victims.

The green kitten

In 1995, a green kitten was born in northwest Denmark. With green fur and even green claws, Miss Greeny made headlines. Sadly for lovers of the bizarre, who dreamed of developing a green breed, vets eventually found that her color was actually verdigris: the local water's high copper content had left a copper patina on the kitten's fur. When Miss Greeny shed, her new coat was normally colored.

The green kitten's color was a temporary effect caused by local water pollution.

fermented sap of giant saguaro cacti, which it slashed open with its blades. The Cactus Cat was a favorite tall story of frontiersmen, never meant to be taken seriously.

Thumper the throwback

Thumper was a kitten born to Manx parents in 1975, but he neither looked nor acted like a normal domestic cat. Despite his undisputed parentage, in appearance, behavior and even voice he seemed wild, adopting the lifestyle of a wildcat and using his huge claws and teeth to hunt his own food. He was identified as a rare genetic throwback to the African Wildcat—the ancestor of our cats way back in Egyptian times.

Japanese dancing cats

In the 1950s, fishermen in the Japanese city of Minamata saw a bad omen when their cats started "dancing"—a frenzied dance that often

FELINE HEROES

Water rescue

When Tim Russell of North Carolina fell off the floating dock where he was working, he trapped his leg and was unable to climb out of the water. His screams for help went unheard—except by his calico cat Toontz, who raced to raise the alarm, making such a commotion that Russell's wife came out to see what was wrong. With the help of passing fishermen, the trapped man was rescued, thanks to Toontz.

Emergency call

Ty, a Siamese cat from British Columbia, saved the life of his owner in July 2004 when she collapsed with heart failure late at night. Ty, whom she had adopted from the SPCA, stayed by her side for more than two hours while she lay drifting in and out of unconsciousness. Persistently licking her face and howling in her ear, he finally revived her sufficiently for her to pick up the phone and dial for help—just in time.

Ty the Siamese received an SPCA Animal Hero Award in 2005 for saving the life of his owner, Myrna Birch.

Fire rescue

There are many records of cats saving their owners by raising the alarm when their houses caught fire. One such was Pantjusha, a cat who lived at the Pantagruel restaurant in Kiev. When the restaurant caught fire, Pantjusha's warning cries saved the lives of owner and clientele. Today his bronze statue stands outside the restaurant to honor his deed.

Pantjusha's statue is one of Kiev's tourist attractions. Legend has it that a local cat once fell in love with the realistic statue.

Guard cat

A burglar who broke into the home of Lynn and John Seeley in 1992 learned not to underrate cats as home protectors. The Seeleys slept peacefully through the break-in until they were woken by the burglar's shriek as their calico cat Aggie defended her home. Before they got downstairs he had fled, leaving only a shoe behind, put to flight by a normally gentle little cat—who also happened to be blind.

Life preserver

Slowly Cat, the pet of Virgil and Linda McMillan of Arkansas, went missing in the depth of winter, with temperatures below -24°C (-12°F). Next day the cat was found behind the house, huddled in an old sack that he refused to leave—because he was curled around an abandoned baby, keeping it warm. The baby was rushed to the hospital, where doctors confirmed that Slowly Cat had saved his life in that bitter cold.

Shadow, from Calgary, Alberta, alerted his sleeping family to deadly carbon monoxide filling their home from a faulty furnace.

David and Goliath

Siamese cross Flash went against the cat's natural flight instinct when he leapt to the defense of his owner. Kelli Kinsman of Massachusetts, five months pregnant, was in her backyard when a large dog attacked her and knocked her down. Before she had time to panic, Flash dashed out and flew at the dog, driving it off in moments although he was only a fraction of its size.

Epilepsy alert

Koutafides, a ginger moggy rescued from life as a stray, rewarded his Australian family by training himself as an epilepsy support cat—a role usually taken by carefully trained dogs. He has the uncanny ability to predict when his master, Rod Pryor, is about to have an epileptic seizure and warn him, staying with him or fetching Rod's wife, Deborah, to his aid if necessary.

Baby's savior

Smokey from South Australia was named Australia's Most Heroic Cat after he saved the life of his owner's one-month-old baby. Dianne Maidment had left her daughter asleep in her crib, but when Smokey started to howl and scratch at the crib, she came running. The baby had stopped breathing, and Smokey's early warning brought help just in time.

CAT-ASTROPHES?

Flooding

A cat in Germany flooded a block of apartments in 2003, when for reasons best known to itself it switched on a shower, then lay down on the drain. Suction trapped him there, blocking the drain while the shower pan filled and overflowed, flooding the apartment and with the water pouring down into the apartments below. The pan was shallow enough for the culprit's head to remain above water, and he was eventually rescued, soggy but unharmed.

When seeking cozy corners, cats make some odd choices. Showers and sinks make fine beds—so long as Puss doesn't knock the taps on!

Postal problems

A fierce ginger cat, from Kent in England, frightened postmen so much they refused to deliver mail to his home. Six-year-old Bat attacked postmen's hands when they pushed letters through the door, and also lay in wait to swipe at their legs. His owner, told to collect his own mail until he could control his "guard cat," explained, "He was a rescue cat and is only little—but he does get stroppy."

Cat burglar

Police called to a break-in at an apartment in Itzsedt, Germany, found the furniture trashed, curtains and window blinds damaged, and an aquarium smashed on the floor. They also found the culprit hiding under a kitchen cabinet—a cat who had found his way in and created havoc. A name tag on his collar enabled them to return him to his owner—with a bill for the damage.

Feline firebugs

Cats and electricity don't always mix well. In 2005, two kittens set fire to their home in Kobe, Japan, by urinating in the fax machine, and the same year a British cat called Felix set fire to his Derbyshire home by vomiting into the television. All three survived unharmed, as did the German cat who set his home in Luedenhausen ablaze in

From Puss in Boots to shoe collector Holly, and not forgetting mischievous kittens, some cats just have a fascination with footwear.

2002 by switching on an electric oven: his appalled mews raised the alarm in time.

Cartoon archvillain

The much-loved cartoon TV series *Earthworm Jim* featured a superhero who was an earth-worm in a high-tech space suit, and an archvillain, Evil the Cat from the planet Heck (complete with sidekick Henchrat). Armed with fangs, claws, and acid-lined hairballs, Evil the Cat strives to destroy the universe with fire and brimstone, and even forces people to listen to elevator music.

A spot of trouble

Spot the ginger tomcat has been barred from almost every pub in Hertford for attacking customers. The 12-year-old cat accompanies his rocker owner everywhere, riding on his shoulders, but his tendency to take a swipe at anyone who got too close made him less than popular down at the pub. The belligerent cat has now exhausted his welcome in some 50 pubs in the town.

Shoe fetishist

A New Zealand cat called Holly spent her nights stealing shoes in her hometown of Manurewa. Having found a pair she liked, she would carry one home, then return for the other to make sure she had a matching pair. With Holly collecting an average of three pairs per night, her owners appealed in the newspapers for locals to come and reclaim their footwear from the boxes stored at their home.

A longtime habitué of the local pubs in Hertford, England, Spot got into a spot of trouble when he became aggressive toward the other regulars.

ROYAL CATS

Cat-loving queen

Queen Victoria, one of the foremost patrons of the National Cat Club and a regular attender at cat shows, was particularly fond of Persians. Her favorite, White Heather, was constantly with her (and after her death in 1901 with her son Edward VII). A staunch supporter of the SPCA, she also cared about the waifs and strays of the feline world, worrying that cats were "generally misunderstood and grossly ill-treated."

As a child, Queen Victoria was brought up with pets, and her beloved cats and dogs remained important to her all her life.

Imperial favorite

Chu Hou-Tsung (1507–66), emperor of China, was inseparable from his favorite cat, Shuang-mei ("Frost-Eyebrows"), who was described as being of "faintly blue" color with "jade-white eyebrows." Upon her death, the royal favorite was buried beneath a stone tablet engraved with the words, "The Grave of a Dragon with Two Horns"—an honor normally reserved for humans of great merit.

Sultan's charity

Sultan El Daher Beybars, 13th-century ruler of Egypt and Syria, was devoted to cats, and in his will he left a garden known as Gheyt-el-Quoltah ("the cats' orchard") in Cairo for the support of homeless cats. The rent of the field was used to provide a daily meal of butchers' scraps for the neighborhood cats, served at the time of afternoon prayer, a tradition that continues to this day.

The stray cats supported by the Sultan may well have been direct descendants of the sacred cats of Ancient Egypt.

Blue blood

Several breeds are claimed by devotees to have been royal favorites in earlier times. The Russian Blue is said to be the royal cat of the Russian czars, and the Siamese, Korat, Burmese, and Khao Manee vie for the title of the "true"

The earliest chroniclers of Siamese cats in the West say explicitly that the breed belonged to Siamese royalty.

terriers. The only member of the royal family to keep cats is Princess Michael of Kent, who favors Burmese and Siamese. Her Burmese cats were apparently not appreciated when they were installed at Kensington Palace, where their loud Oriental voices led to complaints.

The Maine Coon—a tough woodlander, or the descendant of Marie Antoinette's aristo-cats?

royal cat of Siam (modern Thailand). In truth, breed origins are more obscure than explicit and, sadly, breed histories generally owe more to romantic folklore than to historical fact.

Japanese lady-in-waiting

Cat-loving Japanese Emperor Ichijo (980–1011) is sometimes credited with introducing cats to his country. Although this is probably not the case, he certainly awarded cats special treatment and high status. His favorite, Myobu no Otodo ("Chief Lady-in-Waiting of the Inner Palace") was awarded a special rank at court and had human ladies-in-waiting appointed to tend to her needs.

Modern favorites

Today Britain's royal family is definitively associated with dogs rather than cats, from the Queen's corgis to Princess Anne's bull

Courtly Angoras

Angora cats were all the rage at the French court in the 18th century. Louis XV even took his white Angora to Royal Council meetings, letting it play on the table while his ministers talked. Marie Antoinette also kept Angoras, and legend says that after the French Revolution some of her beloved cats were taken to safety in America, where they became the ancestors of the Maine Coon breed.

WHITE HOUSE CATS

Under the cat's thumb

"Rough Rider" Theodore Roosevelt (U.S. President, 1901–09) had cats that rode roughshod over White House visitors. When the President was leading guests from the State Dining Room, they all had to walk around six-toed Slippers, who declined to move out of their way. Tom Quartz, "an exceedingly playful creature," bullied the dogs and liked to waylay human visitors, swatting them as they passed.

Unlucky Angoras

During William McKinley's *(left)* presidency (1897–1901) his wife, Ida, introduced an Angora cat to the White House, naming its kittens after prominent figures. To the President's amusement, the runts of the litter were named Weyler and DeLome, after Spanish dignitaries. These unfortunate kittens were the first casualties when war broke out with Spain, and Ida promptly ordered them drowned.

The Coolidge collection

Calvin Coolidge (1923–29) kept a positive menagerie at the White House, including three cats, Blackie, Tiger, and Bounder. Tiger soon left home, perhaps fed up with the President's sense of humor (which led him to hide Bounder inside cupboards, drawers, and even a grandfather clock to amuse his wife), but Blackie ruled supreme, particularly enjoying riding in the White House elevator.

Driven out by a dog

In 1993, black-and-white Socks accompanied President Bill Clinton to the White House and became the most popular First Cat on record, visiting local hospitals and orphanages and receiving sacks of fan mail. However, when Buddy the Labrador joined the household, Socks did not approve. By 2001, cat and dog were on such bad terms that Socks retired from public life to live with Clinton's former personal secretary.

Socks joined the Clinton household in 1991 as a stray kitten, adopted by Chelsea Clinton when he turned up in her teacher's garden.

Truman's trespasser

Although President Harry Truman (1945–53) was not an animal lover, one cat made determined attempts to move in with him at the White House. Mike the Magicat, "psychic" pet of famous seer Jeane Dixon, arrived uninvited one day and was offered a meal before being driven home to the address on his collar by limousine. Thereafter he had to be collected regularly from the White House gardens by his owner.

Unfortunate name

When George W. Bush was elected to the presidency in 2001, he left one of his cats, six-toed Ernie, behind with a friend in Texas, but brought his black cat India *(above left)* to Washington with him. The cat's name is variously said to derive from her india ink color or from Texas Rangers baseball player, Ruben Sierra, who was nicknamed El Indio, but led to embarrassment for the President when Indian nationalists saw it as an insult to their country and protested.

First Siamese

The first Siamese to reach the United States arrived at the White House in 1878 during the presidency of Rutherford Hayes, a gift to his pet-loving wife, Lucy, from the U.S. consul in Siam. "Siam" survived only 11 months, despite being treated by the President's personal physician, but became a great favorite during her short life. Jimmy Carter and George W. Bush were later also to keep Siamese at the White House.

▲ *Tom Kitten adored Kennedy, which didn't help the President's allergy and sadly led to the cat's departure from the White House.*

Allergic President

President John F. Kennedy (1961–63) and his family kept dogs, rabbits, lambs, ponies, guinea pigs, and hamsters, but his daughter Caroline's cat Tom Kitten stayed only for a short while. Tom Kitten liked the president, but Kennedy was allergic to cats, so Caroline's pet was presented to a secretary and enjoyed life out of the public eye under the new name of Tom Terrific.

FERAL CATS

Slayers or scapegoats?

In parts of the U.S. and Australia, there are drives to exterminate feral cats to protect native wildlife. Environmental groups and cat lovers are locked in heated debate as to whether feral cats devastate wildlife or are being blamed for wildlife losses caused by human impact on the environment. In practice, however, total extermination of this durable species is practically impossible except on small islands.

Rather than endangering wildlife, the Scottish Wildcat is now itself endangered. Once common, it is now restricted to northern Scotland and at risk from both disease and hybridization.

Feral cats are found worldwide. This family is enjoying the sun in a Tunisian marketplace.

Walk on the wild side

Feral cats are domestic cats that have gone wild—strays, discarded pets, and their offspring. They are found worldwide, living in colonies that may be completely independent of humans, or may be supported by local cat lovers. Adult ferals that have never been socialized to humans are usually unable to adapt to pet life, although feral kittens can be tamed if adopted early enough.

Population control

Neutering the members of a colony has proved much more effective in keeping down numbers than any extermination attempts. The neutered cats maintain their territory without producing kittens, so the population remains stable. Destroying resident ferals usually results in an increase in numbers as new arrivals pour in to fill the vacuum and breed prolifically.

Cat-free zone

In 1997, the Tasmanian government launched a $1.2 million program to eradicate feral cats from Macquarie Island, home to several endangered seabird species. Some 2,500 cats were removed from the island, and in 2003 it was officially declared cat-free. The vulnerable seabirds appear to be recovering, but it is now considered necessary to follow up the program by eradicating rodents and rabbits from the island.

Tasmania's offshore islands are home to 20 species of seabird, many in need of protection.

Trap-Neuter-Return

Various charities operate a Trap-Neuter-Return (TNR) program to control the numbers and health of feral cats. The cats are trapped and kittens and tame strays weeded out for adoption before the ferals are vaccinated, neutered, and returned to their colony to live out their lives. Clipping the left ear tip before a cat is released enables workers to identify animals that have been treated.

Employment for ferals

Once trapped and neutered, ferals usually fare best when returned to their established homes. However, in California a Working Cats Program has proved highly successful at relocating neutered and vaccinated ferals to places with a rat problem, ranging from a flower market to a rat-infested Los Angeles police station. The cat patrols have proved cheaper and far more effective than other pest-control methods.

The cats of Rome

Rome's feral cats—an estimated 2,000-odd colonies totaling some 300,000 animals—are luckier than most. In 2001 the city council declared that the cats of the Coliseum, the Forum, and Torre Argentina were to be protected as part of the city's "bio-heritage." Many colonies are fed by local Gattare, or "cat women"; others are tended in the Torre Argentina's underground sanctuary at the spot where Julius Caesar was murdered in 44 B.C.

Cat lovers maintain Rome's vast number of feral cats by feeding them on a regular basis.

HOW WE

SEE CATS

THE CAT IN HERALDRY

The heraldic cat

Cats are not the commonest of heraldic animals, even though their larger relatives (lions, leopards, and tigers) are widespread. They do appear from time to time, as Wildcat, Catamount (a wildcat with tufted ears), or just plain Cat, often symbolizing watchfulness, but sometimes featured as "canting elements" or visual puns, and sometimes referring to some local legend.

A cousin of the catamount, the bobcat appears in the arms of the Special Troops Battalion, 1st Brigade, 3rd Infantry Division of the U.S. Army.

Punning allusion

The coat of arms of the Barony of Windmasters' Hill features references to the word "wind" in its name. These include two aeoli (winds) and also a winged cat ("passant with wings elevated and addorsed," i.e., in a walking position with its wings raised close to its back)—an allusion to Kitty Hawk, site of the first airplane flight.

This shield bears a crowned cat passant, i.e., in walking position with right forepaw raised.

Heraldic felines: Ellesmere Port's Cheshire cat (left) and Katzwang's cat and crozier.

Enduring emblem

A medieval military hero, the Black Prince (Edward Woodstock, Prince of Wales—1330–76) bore the figure of a cat on his war helm as an emblem of watchfulness. Today the

The tabby cat who surmounts the coat of arms of the city of Coventry has a pedigree going back to the 14th century.

city of Coventry, part of which was owned by the Black Prince, still features the cat on its coat of arms, a rather appealing tabby with a suitably watchful expression.

Military emblem

Fierce cats are also popular insignia in the U.S. Army. To take a single example in the American Corps of Engineers, since 1952 the 16th Engineer Battalion have boasted a black cat on their insignia—black in recognition of their nighttime stealth operations. This is a suitably warlike feline, depicted "saliant," in a leaping posture fit for action, and "armed," with claws conspicuously on display.

Don't touch

Several Scottish clans adopted the wildcat as a suitably ferocious emblem, and no fewer than five clans (Mackintosh, Chatton, Gow, MacBain, and MacPherson) share the motto "Touch not the cat but [i.e., without] a glove." This caution against offending warriors well equipped to defend themselves recalls the old Irish motto, "Gentle when stroked, fierce when provoked," which the cat might well adopt.

Catty towns

The coat of arms of Katzwang in Bavaria features a delightful cat (a canting allusion to the town's name) standing on its hind legs and holding a bishop's crozier symbolizing the local abbey. Another Bavarian town, Kasendorf, also features a cat, posed upright and with rather a bemused expression, in reference to the older name of the town, Katzendorf ("cat village").

David Macdonald Stewart's coat of arms may be unique in featuring the distinctive Himalayan cat as its crest.

Feline assortment

Ellesmere Port Borough Council, in Cheshire, has a grinning tabby (a "Cheshire cat') as supporter for its coat of arms, and a former governor of New Zealand based her coat of arms on the theme "a cat among the pigeons" in reference to her career. Modern heraldry now includes specific cat breeds—for example, in 1972, David Macdonald Stewart chose a Himalayan cat holding a tobacco leaf as his crest.

CATS IN RELIGION

Mohammed and Muezza

In Islam, cats are well regarded because tradition says that the Prophet Mohammed was a cat lover. It is said that Mohammed's tabby cat Muezza was one of the few animals to enter paradise. One legend tells how Muezza saved his master from being bitten by a poisonous snake. Another tale tells how, when Muezza fell asleep on the sleeve of his robe, Mohammed cut off his sleeve rather than disturb his pet.

The Judas cat

For many centuries the Christian Church demonized cats. They were agents of the devil, witches' familiars, and symbols of darkness and the occult. In art, a cat hunting mice could represent Satan hunting souls, or even a false priest seeking to "devour" his flock. Italian artists such as Ghirlandaio, Cellini, and Tintoretto included in depictions of the Last Supper a cat seated at the feet of Judas as an icon of perfidy.

Defender of the faith

In Russian tradition, cats were also popularly seen as being on the side of the angels. A folktale tells how the dog and the cat were set to guard the gates of paradise. When the Devil assumed the shape of a mouse and tried to sneak past them, the dog ignored the little creature, but the cat naturally pounced on the mouse and so defended heaven from invasion.

The "Judas cat" attends the traitor Judas Iscariot in The Last Supper, *painted by Jacopo da Ponte Bassano (c. 1517–92).*

Freya's cat-drawn chariot, in Swedish painter *Nils Blommer's* Freya Seeking Her Husband.

Cat of heaven

Hindu legend also tells of the holy cat Patripatan. Sent by his master to fetch a flower from the tree of paradise, Patripatan was delayed there for three centuries because the chief goddess could not bear to part with him. During those centuries the royal court where his master awaited him was untouched by time, and Patripatan finally returned to them in a blaze of glory bearing a whole branch of the sacred tree.

Patron saint

Cats have their own patron saints. St. Gertrude of Nivelles is the official patron of both cats and gardeners, but in southwestern France St. Agatha took over the role because the Languedoc form of her name, Santo Gato, translates as "Saint Cat." On St. Agatha's Day (February 5), she was said to appear in the form of an angry cat to women who failed to honor her feast day by refraining from work.

Norse cats

In Norse mythology, the fertility goddess Freya rides in a chariot drawn by two great cats. Given the cat's outstanding fertility, it seems an appropriate choice, although some experts believe that Freya's beasts were not domestic cats but their far less fecund cousins, lynxes. Those who favor cats for the role argue that these would have been Norwegian Forest Cats, a breed that evolved in the Norse world.

The cat in the manger

Popular Christian tradition also included a kinder view of the cat. According to medieval legend, a stable cat was present at the birth of Christ, and snuggled in the manger to keep the baby Jesus warm. The Virgin Mary blessed the cat for its kindness, and marked her initial on its forehead—hence the "M" marking on the head of tabby cats to this day.

"M" for Mary is written as a sign of the Virgin's blessing on the tabby's forehead.

FELINE FOLKLORE

King of the Cats

According to Scottish folklore, cats have a king. The story goes that a young man was telling his friend of a strange sight he had seen: a feline funeral procession, with cats carrying a crowned coffin to the grave. Before he could complete his story, a cat sitting in the room with them leapt up crying, "By Jove! Old Peter's dead—and I'm the king of the cats!," dashed up the chimney, and was seen no more.

Black cats are often traditionally held to have supernatural powers. In Finland, they were thought to carry the souls of the dead to the Otherworld.

The Christmas Cat

Icelandic tradition holds that anyone who doesn't have at least one new garment to wear for Christmas will be taken by the monstrous Yule Cat (Jólaköttur). In olden times, everyone was rewarded with clothing for getting the autumn wool spun and woven before Christmas, so the Yule Cat threatened only the idle who had neglected their work.

Cats and the dead

Folklore from many countries holds that cats should be kept away from the dead. There was a widespread belief that a cat left with a human corpse would eat the face. Transylvanians believed that a corpse would become a vampire if a cat jumped over it, and the Scots held that any cat that entered the room where a dead body lay must be killed; otherwise the first person to touch the cat would go blind.

Cats are often said to be able to see spirits and fairies. In this illustration by Francis Gilbert Attwood for The Fairies' Festival *(1895), an amiable cat is visited by a totally unthreatening elf, but in many tales the relationship has more sinister implications.*

Vampire cat

Spanish-Jewish legend tells of El Broosha, a black vampire cat that comes by night to suck the blood of sleeping babies. El Broosha is identified with Lilith, the first wife of Adam, who refused to accept her destined role and flew away. When angels threatened to punish her by destroying her descendants, Lilith swore to attack Adam's descendants, which in this version of the story she does in cat form.

In the folklore of witchcraft, black cats may be familiar spirits supplied by Satan, or even witches themselves in feline form.

Fairy cat

In the Scottish Highlands, watch out for the fairy cat Cath Sith, described as being the size of a dog and completely black save for a white spot on its breast. A ferocious beast with arched back and bristling fur, Cait Sith is said to attack those who disturb it. The ancestor of this mythical beast was probably the notoriously fierce Scottish Wildcat, or perhaps the big black wildcat/domestic cat hybrid known as Kellas Cats.

Magical matagots

French peasants believed in matagots, magician cats that brought wealth to their owners if they were treated well. If you were lucky enough to find one, you had to lure it to you with a plump chicken, carry it home without ever looking back, and thereafter give it the first taste of every meal. In return, it would give its owner a gold coin every morning.

A useful spell

If a black cat crosses your path, always be polite. To bring good luck, stroke the cat three times while reciting this charm:

Black cat, cross my path,
Good fortune bring to home and hearth.
When I am away from home,
Bring me luck wherever I roam.

If you prefer bad luck, insulting the cat instead will bring this about.

A different tradition claims that a black cat crossing your path is an omen of danger ahead, so instead of chatting to the cat it might be to safer to turn back.

CATS AND WITCHCRAFT

The age of witchcraft

Independent, night walking, and moon eyed, cats inevitably appeared to the superstitious medieval church as pagan creatures. From about 1100 to about 1700, witch hunters claimed that the devil manifested himself in the form of a cat, and that witches both transformed themselves into cats and kept demonic "familiar spirits," supplied by Satan, in cat form.

The 1692 Salem witchcraft trials accused 19 witches (and their cats) of occult practices.

Familiars

By the 16th century the cat was firmly established in popular lore as the witch's familiar. During the infamous witch trials, torture forced many victims to plead guilty to charges of witchcraft and to identify their pets as familiars. Feline familiars mentioned in trial records include Sathan ("a whyte spotted Catte"), Tyttey ("a little grey Cat"), Gille ("a Blacke Catte"), and Ginnie ("a Kitlyng").

Cats are often depicted as witches' "familiars"—demons that attend them when called to do so.

In film and fiction

Witches' cats are popular fictional characters today, from Salem, the talking black cat from the TV series *Sabrina, the Teenage Witch,* to Gobbolino the Witch's Cat in Ursula Moray Williams's children's book of that name. One of the most notable is Greebo, Nanny Ogg's appalling and endearing tomcat in Terry Pratchett's series of Discworld novels, a malevolent one-eyed scrapper whose owner still sees him as a dear little kitten.

Household guardians

Hundreds of years ago, the ancient custom of sacrificing a living creature to safeguard the foundations of a new building lingered on in the occasional practice of entombing a cat in the walls. Naturally mummified cats have been discovered in old houses all over Europe. Some may have been accidentally trapped during building works, but others appear to have been put there deliberately to drive off evil spirits.

Ulrich Molitor was a German professor who wrote a treatise on witchcraft in 1489. It included this woodcut showing a wizard being taken to a sabbat by a demon cat.

Shape-shifters

Witches were believed to be able to shape-change into animal form, often that of a cat, to carry out their evil work. seventeenth-century Scottish "witch" Isabel Gowdie revealed the magic formula she used to turn herself into a cat, which was to repeat this verse:

"I shall go intill ane catt,
With sorrow, and sych, and a blak shott;
And I sall goe in the Divellis nam,
Ay will I come hom againe."

Black cat mojo

In African-American hoodoo, gamblers burn candles in the shape of a black cat to bring luck at cards, and "root doctors" hold that every black cat has one special bone that can restore lost lovers or grant invisibility. The black cat's bone is valued as a powerful mojo (amulet)—but nowadays "black cat mojos" sold commercially are more likely to be chicken bones painted black.

Lady Ann

At the tomb of Lady Ann Smith of Edmondthorpe, Leicestershire, who died in 1652, her statue bears a strange red stain on its wrist. Tradition says she was a witch who turned herself into a huge black cat. One night

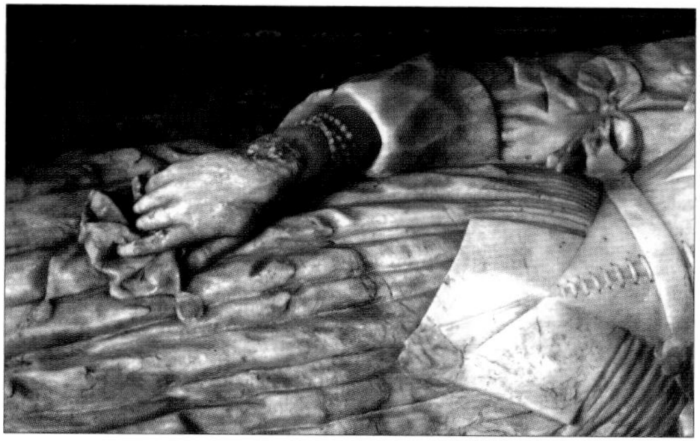

The red stain on the wrist of Lady Ann Smith's effigy is reputed to be evidence of the injury she suffered while in the form of a cat.

her butler struck the cat on the paw with a cleaver. It vanished, but next day Lady Ann displayed a wounded wrist. The cat's bloodstains remained on the kitchen floor until 1920, when the flagstones were taken up.

CAT SUPERSTITIONS

Good and bad luck

A black cat crossing your path means good luck in England, but bad luck in the U.S.

A stray cat coming to your house brings good luck—unless you drive it away, which will bring bad luck.

Cats found lurking in coal mines mean bad luck.

In the theater, cats backstage bring good luck—but bad luck if they step onstage.

Letting a cat look in a mirror will bring trouble to you.

Find one white hair on a black cat, and Lady Luck will smile on you.

Nelson, Winston Churchill's lucky black cat, was outside 10 Downing Street on the day war with Germany was declared in September 1939.

Weather forecasters

A cat sneezing means rain is coming.

A cat sitting with its back to the fire means there will be frost that night.

A cat licking its fur against the grain means there will be hail.

Toasting their backs at the fire, these cats forecast frost—or just like to keep warm.

A cat putting its paw behind its ear when washing means there will be rain.

A cat sleeping with all four paws tucked underneath it means cold weather ahead.

Cats running around wildly foretell a wind.

In sickness and in health

If a cat leaves home while a member of the family is sick, that person will die.

A stye on the eye can be cured by stroking it with the tail of a black cat.

A wart can be cured by smearing three drops of cat's blood on it.

A dried cat's skin held to the face cures toothache.

Wash a sick person and throw the water over a cat, and the cat will carry the sickness away with it.

When a cat sneezes three times, its owner will catch a cold.

Kick a cat, and you will suffer from rheumatism in that leg.

Dreams

Dream of a white cat: good luck is on its way.
Dream of a black and white cat: you will be lucky with children.
Dream of a ginger cat: you will be lucky with money.
Dream of a tortoiseshell cat: you will be lucky in love.
Dream of a tabby cat: you will be lucky with your home.
Dream of a multicolored cat: you will have luck making friends.
Dream of a cat mewing: beware a false friend.
Dream of two cats fighting: expect illness or a quarrel.
Pluck a whisker from a dreaming cat, place it under your pillow, and that night you will dream what the cat was dreaming.

Love and marriage

If an unmarried girl accidentally steps on a cat's tail, she will be married within 12 months.
If in doubt whether to accept a proposal, fold three hairs from a cat's tail into a paper and leave it on the doorstep overnight. In the morning, the hairs will have formed into Y for Yes or N for No.
A cat sneezing near the bride-to-be on the morning of her wedding day means that she will have a happy life.
If the family cat attends a wedding, it brings good luck.

Daily life

If the first thing you see upon waking up is cats playing, the rest of the day will be wasted.
A cat washing its face at the front door means company coming.
If a cat scratches you, you will be disappointed that day.

Unlucky 13

Seating 13 at the table is traditionally unlucky, but at London's Savoy Hotel diners are saved from the risk by Kaspar, the lucky black cat. Kaspar was carved out of wood by Basil Ionides in 1926, and since then has been the 14th guest for any parties of 13, seated on his own chair with a napkin tied around his neck. His company has been enjoyed by such famous guests as Winston Churchill.

After a tragedy in 1898 at the end of a Savoy dinner party for 13 guests, a staff member joined all such parties, until Kaspar took over.

URBAN MYTHS

Modern folklore

Urban myths are stories that spread from teller to teller, often thought to be true but rarely traceable back to any evidence and often developing further as they are passed on—a kind of modern folklore. Perhaps the earliest feline urban myth is the tale that cats suck babies' breath and therefore must never be allowed near the cradle. Others are more complicated.

Another "cat up a tree" urban myth tells of the cat who is rescued by the fire department—and then run over by the departing fire engine.

Answer to prayer

A favorite urban myth is the tale of the vicar's cat that gets stuck up a tree. Using a rope to try to pull down the branch where the cat is perched, the vicar accidentally catapults his pet over the rooftops. Weeks later, a parishioner tells him proudly of her little miracle: her son was remarking how much he wanted a cat when one fell out of the sky into his lap, clearly an answer to prayer!

Substitute cat

Another tale going the rounds is that of the airport baggage handler who discovers that a cat being flown out in a crate is dead. To avoid blame, he swaps the corpse for a stray cat of the same color and loads it on the plane. When it arrives alive and kicking, the owner is so shocked she faints—her own cat had died just before departure, and she was shipping its body home for burial.

Substitution again

In a variant of this tale, a cat breeder arranges to import a valuable stud cat from the U.S. The cat's plane makes an overnight stop at Havana, where one of the airport staff lets it out of its crate to stretch its legs and it disappears. In a panic, he grabs—yes, you guessed!—a stray cat of the same color, pops it in the crate, and sends it off the next morning. The punch line is that the breeder never queries the substitute.

Fatal foot lickers

A few years ago, an alarming tale of cats killing their owners by licking their feet spread across

America. Overly enthusiastic cats were said to be nibbling too hard and drawing blood, with sleeping owners failing to notice the wound and bleeding to death. The myth had a huge effect when it was broadcast on a radio program in July 2002, and frightened owners flooded cat shelters with unwanted pets.

Social embarrassment

A widespread tale is of the hostess who tests some slightly dubious chicken on her cat before a party. The cat seems fine, so she serves the food to her guests. No sooner have they left than she finds the cat yowling in agony, so she hastily phones all her guests to warn them to have their stomachs pumped. When she returns to the cat, however, she finds it is simply having kittens...

Cat-flap crisis

Magnetically operated cat flaps inspire stories of cats struggling home with sets of cutlery stuck to their magnetic collars. The classic tale is that of the couple who come home to find their kittens in the role of fridge magnets, stuck to the fridge door by their collars. Despite the popularity of such stories, low magnet strength and elastic safety inserts in such collars make them highly improbable.

Reluctant homing cat

This one is a spin on tales of incredible homing cats. A cat owner, fed up with his cat's "unsanitary habits," rehomed it with friends a few miles away. The cat seemed to settle down, but one day he came home to find it on his doorstep. Touched by its loyalty, he resolved to keep it. He was less impressed when a friend explained that he had spotted the cat on the other side of town and, despite its protests, carried it "home."

GHOST CATS

Civil War Ghost

During the American Civil War, Tom Cat, mascot at Fort McAllister, Georgia, kept up the troops' spirits by scampering along the ramparts dodging cannon shot and musket balls. His luck ran out in March 1863 when a stray shot from Union forces hit him. But to this day, staff and visitors claim to see Tom Cat's ghost running around the fort and feel an invisible cat rubbing against their legs.

Set in feudal Japan, Black Cat in the Forest *blends folk tradition with modern horror story.*

Cats and the supernatural are irrevocably linked in folklore and superstition.

Vampire ghosts

In Japanese folklore, ghost cats are often spirits of murdered women returned in feline form to avenge their deaths. Today *kaibyo* (ghost-cat) horror films are a popular Japanese genre. Classics include Kaneto Shindo's *Black Cat in the Forest* (1968) and Tokuzo Tanaka's *The Haunted Castle* (1969), in both of which ghost cats wreak vengeance upon the samurai who caused their deaths.

Haunted lighthouse

Workers at the Fairport Harbor Lighthouse in Ohio, who had for years reported seeing—and feeling—a ghost cat in the dark tower, felt vindicated when renovation work in 2000 uncovered a mummified gray cat under the basement. Apparently the pet of a former lighthouse keeper's had trapped itself in a crawl space under the floor. Its remains are now on display in the lighthouse museum.

Horned cat ghost

In 1943, British clairvoyant John Pendragon investigated a London house said to be haunted by a monstrous horned cat. He concluded that black magic had been practiced there, involving the sacrifice of cats, before the perpetrator had hanged himself. Locals confirmed that a previous resident had indeed hanged himself in the house—and that before his death they had heard cats yowling there in the middle of the night.

Curse of the cat mummy

Another mummified cat is a permanent resident at the Old Mill Hotel, Sudbury, Suffolk, England. Uncovered by builders in 1971, it was evidently bricked up alive to ward off evil spirits when the mill was built. Whenever it has been removed, fires, floods, and other disasters have followed.

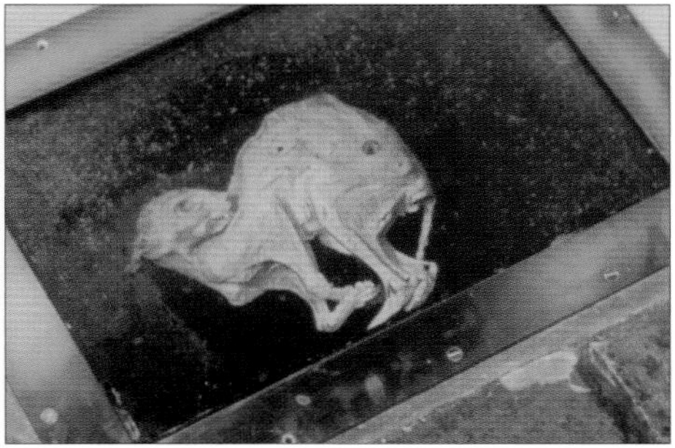

Restored to its place under the floorboards, the mysterious mummy guards the Old Mill.

The ghost cat of the Capitol is said to grow huge before people's eyes, then disappear.

An art store where it was displayed burned down, leaving the cat unharmed among the ashes. The mummy has now been replaced under the floorboards, and all seems well.

Bad luck in the Capitol

The United States Capitol building in Washington has its share of ghosts, including a Civil War soldier and a worker carrying a tray. There is also a ghost cat in the basement, sightings of which are said to foretell a national disaster. It was seen in the late 1930s just before the stock market crashed, and again before President Kennedy's assassination.

Classic ghost story

In M. R. James's classic ghost story *The Stalls of Barchester Cathedral* (1911), a carved wooden cat comes to life to haunt Archdeacon Haynes and leads him to his death. The carving bears a curse, "Who that touches me with his Hand, If a Bloody hand he bear I councell him to be ware," and Dr. Haynes had achieved his position by causing the death of his predecessor.

FAIRY STORIES AND FABLES

The fox and the cat

Aesop told a fable of a fox who boasted to a cat that he had hundreds of tricks to defeat his enemies. The cat had only one, but reckoned that enough. When a pack of hounds came upon them, the cat shot up a tree to safety, but the fox took so long deciding which plan to adopt that the hounds caught him. The moral: Better one trick you can rely on than a hundred on which you can't.

Perched safely in his tree, the cat watches while the fox discovers to his cost that quick thinking beats over-cleverness hands down.

Belling the cat

Another well-known Aesop fable tells how the mice met in council to decide how to keep the cat from catching them. One bright mouse suggested tying a bell around the cat's neck to warn of her approach. The other mice thought this a great idea, except one, who pointed out the snag: Who was going to attach the bell? The moral: It's easy to suggest impossible solutions, harder to carry them out.

Dick Whittington's cat

In this English folktale based on the life of Richard Whittington (c.1350–1423), four times Lord Mayor of London, a poor country boy seeking his fortune in London finds it when he sends his cat abroad with a trader. The cat deals with a plague of mice for the King of Barbary, who sends back payment in gold. However, the real Whittington's wealth probably came via a type of merchant ship termed a "cat" rather than an actual feline.

One of the best-loved fairy-tale characters, Puss in Boots is cleverer than his master.

Puss in boots

Charles Perrault (1628–1703) gave us the popular tale of the poor man who was given a cat by his father. The talking cat employs his cunning to win his master fine clothes, then a castle, and finally the hand of the king's daughter in marriage. A popular pantomime character, Puss In Boots recently acquired a new lease on life from his role in the animated film *Shrek II*, voiced by Antonio Banderas.

Why the cat kills rats

In this Nigerian folktale, the King of Calabar lived with a cat for his housekeeper and a rat for his

Cats' ratting abilities are often exaggerated: few cats will tackle a full-grown rat.

houseboy. The rat fell in love with a servant girl, and started stealing gifts for her from the king's stores. The cat was in trouble, for it was her responsibility to take care of the storeroom. When she found out who was to blame, she killed the rat—and cats have been angry with rats ever since.

Why cats chase dogs

An American folktale says that long ago Dog was married to Cat. They lived happily at first, but then Cat said she was too ill to cook for Dog when he came home from work. Next day Dog pretended to go off to work, but hid in the house to find out if she was really ill. When he saw that she wasn't, but spent the day playing with Kitten, he lost his temper and chased her around the house—and he has never forgiven her.

Kisa the cat

In the Icelandic folktale of Kisa the Cat, the Princess Ingibjorg is captured by a giant who cuts off her feet. The enchanted cat Kisa comes to her rescue, retrieves the feet, and magically reattaches them. For her reward she asks to sleep at the foot of Ingibjorg's bed on her wedding night, which breaks the enchantment upon her and returns her to human shape, to live happily ever after as a princess.

Kisa comes to the rescue of the footless Ingibjorg, driving a cart and using her own tail as a whip to make the horse go faster.

CATS IN LITERATURE

The monk's cat

In the ninth century an Irish monk at the Austrian monastery of Carinthia took a break from his labors over St. Paul's Epistles to jot down a poem about his cat Pangur Ban ("White Pangur") on the margins of the gospel, comparing his task of hunting words with the cat's task of hunting mice. The monk's name is now long forgotten, but that of his feline companion lives on—the first cat to appear in Western literature.

My Cat Jeoffry

Eighteenth-century poet Christopher Smart *(left)* spent years of his life in a cell in the London madhouse of Bedlam, with his cat Jeoffry his only comfort. He celebrated their friendship in a long, mystical poem that begins, "For I will consider my cat Jeoffry," pondering points from the practical ("For by stroaking of him I have found out electricity") to the spiritual ("For I perceived God's light about him both wax and fire").

Tactless Tobermory

In his 1909 short story *Tobermory*, satirist Saki (Hector Hugh Munro) depicts one of the most autocratic felines in fiction. Taught human speech by an eccentric German professor, Tobermory proceeds to wreck a country house party by revealing all the embarrassing secrets he has overheard before, to the relief of all, he dies "in unequal combat with the big Tom from the Rectory."

Creator of Archie and Mehitabel, Don Marquis (right) with his first wife, Reina, and author Ellis Parker Butler, photographed in 1912.

Mehitabel the alley cat

U.S. humorist Don Marquis's exuberant verse saga of Archy the cockroach (a reincarnated free-verse poet) and Mehitabel the cat (self-proclaimed reincarnation of Cleopatra) first appeared in New York newspapers in 1916 and ran to nearly 500 sketches. Low on morals but high on morale, alley-cat Mehitabel sticks to the motto, "Toujours gai!" through the trials, tribulations, and kittens of her Bohemian life.

Demonic Behemoth

In Mikhail Bulgakov's surreal Russian masterpiece, *The Master and Margarita*, one of the principal characters is the huge black cat

This portrait of Mikhail Bulgakov, creator of the demonic Behemoth, partners him with a suitably sinister owl-faced feline.

Behemoth, trickster servant of the Devil and addicted to chess and vodka. Although he shares his name (Russian "hippopotamus") with the demon rated as cup bearer to Satan, Behemoth was inspired by the author's pet, Flyushka (also huge, but gray).

Discworld swaggerer

Greebo the tomcat is one of the best-loved characters in Terry Pratchett's series of Discworld novels. His owner, Nanny Ogg, insists that he is a dear little thing, but what the rest of the world sees is a malevolent thug who chases wolves and eats vampires. In later books he sometimes, reluctantly, takes on human form, radiating menace and sexuality while still trying to wash behind his ears with a paw.

Gallico's cats

The prolific output of U.S. writer Paul Gallico (1897–1976) included two popular feline fantasy novels. *Jennie* (1950) tells the story of a motherly stray who adopts a lost boy after he has been turned into a cat. In *Thomasina: The Cat Who Thought She Was God* (1957—filmed in 1964 as *The Three Lives of Thomasina*), the near-death experience of the cat brings her into the world of cat goddess Bubastis.

Paul Gallico reads his story Ludmila *to Elke Alberle, who plays the part of Ludmila in the film, and Baroness Ludmila Von Falz-Fein (right), to whom he dedicated his book.*

CHILDREN'S BOOKS

The Cheshire Cat

Everyone knows the Cheshire Cat from Lewis Carroll's *Alice in Wonderland* (1865), with his cheesy grin and his ability to appear and disappear at will. It is less well known that he was not Carroll's invention. The expression "grin like a Cheshire cat" is a lot older than Alice and of unknown origin—various theories link it to a local cheesemaker's stamp, a stone carving, or a medieval outlaw called Caterling.

Alice contemplates the Cheshire Cat, and his grin. Soon the cat will disappear, leaving only his smile floating on the air.

Mike Myers played the Cat in the Hat in the 2003 film, which extended the story considerably—and was panned by critics.

Magical mayhem

The Cat in the Hat (1957), the tale of an anarchic cat who transforms a dull afternoon into mayhem, was produced by Theodor Seuss Geisel (better known to the world as Dr. Seuss) as a primer based on a mere 225-word vocabulary for new readers. The top-hatted cat established Dr. Seuss as a key figure in children's books before going on to a sequel, a TV animated series, and a film starring Mike Myers in the title role.

From Beatrix to Harry

J.K. Rowling's best-selling series about young wizard Harry Potter began in 1997, but it was not until 1999, with *Harry Potter and the Prisoner of Azkaban*, that the ginger cat Crookshanks made his appearance. He belongs to Harry's friend Hermione Granger and plays an active part in their adventures, as he has more than normal cat intelligence, being part kneazle (a magical catlike creature with big ears and a lion's tail).

The cat that walked by himself

One of the best-loved *Just So Stories* of Rudyard Kipling (1865–1936), this fable tells how the cat became domesticated. Unlike Dog, Horse, and Cow, who abandon freedom in exchange for care and food, Cat joins Man's household on his own terms after some hard bargaining: "I am not a friend and I am not a servant, I am the cat who walks by himself and I wish to come into your cave."

Kipling's own illustration shows the Cat "walking on his wild lone through the Wet Wild Woods."

Not just Peter Rabbit

The tales of Beatrix Potter (1866–1943), creator of Peter Rabbit, include some memorable cats. Her animals are really people in cat form, much of their charm lying in her meticulously observed drawings: Tom Kitten (*The Tale of Tom Kitten*, 1907) is any naughty little boy, his mother, Tabitha Twitchet, is every harassed mother, and Ginger the store-keeping cat (*The Tale of Ginger and Pickles*, 1909) is equally human.

Orlando the Marmalade Cat

Orlando was the hero of a series of 19 illustrated books written and illustrated by Kathleen Hale between 1938 and 1972. With his wife, Grace, and their three kittens, Pansy, Blanche, and the mischievous Tinkle—the latter based on Hale herself as a child—Orlando enjoys a range of adventures, from a seaside vacation to a trip to the North Pole to see Santa Claws and a visit to the moon.

The Amazing Maurice

What happens when Terry Pratchett crosses the Pied Piper with his fantasy Discworld is the award-winning *Amazing Maurice and His Educated Rodents* (2001), in which piper, rats, and townspeople dance to the tune of Maurice the talking cat. Resolutely self-centered, Maurice has designed a money-spinning scam in which the bewildered rats cooperate, but finds he can manipulate them only so far...

CAT DETECTIVES

Mystery

Detective fiction with a feline bias has become a recognizable genre since the 1960s, with cats featuring as clues, eyewitnesses, main characters, and even sleuths. American author Lilian Jackson Braun, who is credited with originating the trend, explains its success as follows: "not all mystery fans may like cats, [but] all cat-fanciers seem to like mysteries."

Siamese duo

Lilian Jackson Braun's trendsetting mystery series *The Cat Who...* began in 1966 with *The Cat Who Could Read Backwards* and now comprises nearly 30 titles in which the unforgettable Siamese duo Koko and Yum Yum assist reporter Jim Qwilleran in his detective work. Braun shares her home with two Siamese, and indeed started writing cat stories to console herself after the death of her first of this breed.

Midnight Louie

Carole Nelson Douglas's series of mystery stories, beginning with *Catnap* (1992), features a hard-boiled feline private investigator, Midnight Louie the jet-black tomcat, who both assists his human partner, Temple Barr, in her detective work, and investigates crime among cats. Since 1996 cat-loving Douglas has combined bookstore signings with cat shelter promotions in the Midnight Louie Adopt-a-Cat tours.

Big Mike

Another cat detective series is written by Garrison Allen (pseudonym of Gary Amo), who lives in California with his black cat Oliver. His novels, including *Desert Cat, Baseball Cat,* and *Dinosaur Cat*, feature mystery bookstore owner Penny Warren and her intrepid assistant, the Abyssinian cat Mycroft, "Big Mike," who track down local murderers together.

Winky

Evan Marshall is creator of a popular mystery series featuring literary agent and part-time

CAROLE NELSON DOUGLAS
Cat in an Orange Twist
"Midnight Louie is the funniest, hairiest, hard-boiled PI on the planet."—JANET EVANOVICH

Carole Nelson Douglas combines feline whimsy with a clear-eyed look at a range of contemporary issues.

sleuth Jane Stuart and her brilliant tortoiseshell cat Winky, beginning with *Missing Marlene* (1999). Winky, who usually plays a key part in helping Jane solve her mysteries, is closely based on a real cat of that name that the author once owned.

Francis

Akif Pirincci's *Felidae* trilogy is a set of crime novels written from a cat's perspective, in which the cat Francis has to solve a mysterious series of feline murders in his neighborhood. The first novel, *Felidae* (1989), was translated into at least 17 languages and produced as an animated film, and was followed by *Felidae II* (1993) and *Cave Canem* (1999).

Joe Grey and Dulcie

Shirley Rousseau Murphy's *Joe Grey Mysteries*, inspired by a real gray-and-white kitten called Joe Grey, have won six national Cat Writers' Association Awards and star crime-solving feline Joe Grey and his friend Dulcie. Joe and Dulcie are no ordinary cats, for they understand and speak human language—though Joe likes to stay anonymous, and reports his findings to the police in the form of a mystery voice on the phone.

Shirley Rousseau Murphy has won seven Muse Medallions from the Cat Writers Association for her Joe Grey series.

Moggy miscellany

Other authors who find cats and crime mix well together include Rita Mae Brown, who shares credit with her cat Sneaky Pie for her mystery stories starring Mrs. Murphy the feline sleuth, Lydia Adamson, with more than 20 cat-centered titles to her credit since *A Cat in the Manger* (1990), and Marian Babson, many of whose novels such as *Diamond Cat* and *Murder at the Cat Show* include cats as major, and very sympathetic, characters.

CATS IN FILM AND TELEVISION

Silent star

The first feline Hollywood star was Pepper, way back in the days of silent movies. This little gray cat appeared in several films, acting with such famous figures as Charlie Chaplin, Fatty Arbuckle, and the Keystone Kops.

Temperamental star

During a 12-year acting career, Orangey, a ginger tabby, starred in such films as *Rhubarb* (1952) and *Breakfast at Tiffany's* (1961) and twice won the Patsy Award for Best Animal Actor. Acclaimed as one of the most talented animal actors in the world, he was also notorious as one of the most temperamental—in fact, one of his reluctant colleagues described him as "the World's Meanest Cat."

Talented but temperamental Orangey with co-star Audrey Hepburn in Breakfast at Tiffany's.

Cat versus alien

In the trailblazing science fiction/horror film *Alien* (1979), the sinister alien stowaway aboard a doomed spaceship destroys all but two crew members—one being Jones the cat. Feline common sense and survival tactics, along with a devoted owner, enable the orange tabby to make it safely to the end of the film, unlike most of the mere humans aboard.

To boldly go

Cat-loving *Star Trek* addicts were no doubt delighted that the 1987 series *Star Trek: The Next Generation* featured a cat, Spot, aboard the starship *Enterprise*. With little regard for continuity, Spot changed sex and also breed within the series (starting out as a Somali, and later becoming a ginger shorthair), variations that the *Star Trek Encyclopedia* kindly credits to a matter transporter accident.

Galactic guardian

Orion the cat has a key part to play in the 1997 sci-fi comedy movie *Men in Black*. Government agents assigned to retrieve a whole galaxy stolen by an intergalactic terrorist know that it is hidden "in Orion's belt"—but this turns out to be not the constellation but the collar of Orion the cat.

Orion in Men in Black, *seen here with the stolen galaxy hanging from his collar, is an alien's pet—but it is never specified whether he himself is an alien, or an earth cat.*

The ginger-and-white cat playing the role of Orion is one of the most expressive feline actors to appear on the screen.

Furry Shakespeareans

In 1989, Belgian director Armando Acosta created a version of *Romeo and Juliet* acted entirely by cats, with narration by John Hurt and with music from Prokofiev's *Romeo and Juliet* score. Some 150 street cats from Venice, Ghent, and New York (with a beautiful white Angora playing Juliet) were filmed acting naturally on the sets, and 5,000 hours of editing later Acosta had a stunning feline rendition of Shakespeare's story.

Feline inspiration

British actor Andy Serkis, who played the part of creepy, pitiful Gollum in the *Lord of the Rings* trilogy, found the voice for his character by listening to his cats. Serkis's cats produced just the right sound for Gollum's throaty gurgles when they were coughing up fur balls. Unfortunately, imitating the sound was hard on a human throat, and Serkis had to drink endless honey and lemon to keep his voice going.

Sophisti-cat

Talking black cat Salem starred in the TV fantasy comedy series *Sabrina, the Teenage Witch* (1996–2003). Not quite the traditional witch's familiar, Salem was a warlock transformed into feline form as a punishment for trying to take over the world. A sophisticated character who patronized Internet chat rooms, operating a laptop computer with a pencil held in his mouth, he was played by four different cats plus animatronic puppets that supplemented the feline stars.

The four cats who played Salem each had their own specialties. Elvis was the one who does the "talking," with appropriate mouth movements.

CARTOON CATS

Krazy Kat

Originally a minor player in George Harriman's newspaper cartoon strip *The Dingbat Family*, Krazy Kat acquired his own strip in 1913, and three years later made the transition from paper to film to become the very first animated cartoon cat. His slapstick relationship with the aggressive Ignatz Mouse set the tone for generations of cat-and-mouse cartoons.

Felix

Initially inspired by Kipling's *The Cat Who Walked by Himself*, Felix the Cat was the creation of Australian cartoonist Pat Sullivan. His first appearance in *Feline Follies* (1919) was soon followed by others, and he became the world's most popular cartoon character until the arrival of Mickey Mouse. His screen career led to comic books, strips, and TV series as well as the popular song *Felix Kept On Walking*.

Sylvester

Star of numerous Warner Brothers cartoons, black-and-white Sylvester made his debut in *Life with Feathers* (1945) and spent his time failing to capture Tweety Pie the canary. His animated figure was inspired by jowly executive producer Johnny Burton.

Sylvester is one of Warner Bros.'s most memorable creations.

Mel Blanc, who voiced the part, once commented that Sylvester's thick lisp made him spray so much saliva that he advised other cast members to wear raincoats.

Underground icons

Cats aren't always perfect, and their "dark side" inspired two notable anti-establishment feline characters popular in 1960s underground comics, Robert Crumb's fast-talking, sex-obsessed Fritz the Cat, and Gilbert Shelton's slobbish creation Fat Freddy's Cat, an orange tabby tomcat who lives with a trio of stoned hippies, the Fabulous Furry Freak Brothers.

Heathcliff—no hero

George Gately's comic strip about fat orange cat Heathcliff first appeared in 1973 and is now syndicated in more than 1,000 newspapers. Named, tongue in cheek, after the romantic hero of *Wuthering Heights*, Heathcliff is a self-centered household despot whose egotistical antics rang a bell with many cat owners. From 1980 Heathcliff also appeared in a television series, and in 1986 in a feature-length film.

Doraemon

Japan's favorite cartoon cat is Doraemon, a robot cat from the future who has traveled back in time to ensure that his employers' feckless ancestor becomes a success instead of leaving his descendants mountains of debt. Doraemon's main technological edge is a four-dimensional pocket packed with gadgets, and his cat nature appears in his hatred of rats and mice (which he tackles with a nuclear bomb from his pocket).

Top Cat and his gang of Manhattan alley cats always get the better of hapless Officer Dibble.

Top Cat

A Hanna-Barbera cartoon dating back to 1961, Top Cat (also known as Boss Cat) was inspired by the Sergeant Bilko character from the satirical comedy *You'll Never Get Rich*. Throughout the 30 episodes Top Cat and his gang of alley cats plan elaborate, and inevitably unsuccessful, get-rich scams from their garbage-can home near the police station, while the local patrolman tries equally unsuccessfully to evict them.

Garfield

Another feline antihero, Garfield, was created by Jim Davis, named after his grandfather, and based on the farm cats with which Davis grew up. Sarcastic, lazy, and addicted to lasagne, Garfield runs rings around his owner, Jon Arbuckle, and the rather dim dog Odie. His first newspaper strip appeared in 1978, and in 2004 he hit the big screen with *Garfield: The Movie*.

A computer-generated Garfield encounters a canine actor as Odie (a role shared by two Dachshund mixes) in Garfield: The Movie.

CATS IN ART

Sinister cats

In medieval and Renaissance art, the predatory cat often symbolizes evil, in varying degrees. A cat stalking a caged goldfinch represents the Devil vainly stalking the infant Jesus, or a cat at the feet of Judas foretells his role. In Hieronymus Bosch's *Garden of Earthly Delights* (post-1500), the cat catching a mouse in the Garden of Eden foreshadows the moment when Adam is "caught" by Eve and her apple.

God creates Eve in Bosch's Garden of Earthly Delights, *but prophetically the cat has a mouse.*

Sacred cats

The Virgin Mary is often depicted with a cat, symbolic or naturalistic. Sometimes it is hard to say which. In Lorenzo Lotto's *Annunciation* (c.1527), a tabby cat is shocked by the appearance of the Angel Gabriel—evil fleeing God's messenger, or a delightful touch of

Leonardo's drawing of the Virgin and Child, who holds a distracted cat in his arms.

realism? However, often the cat appears as part of the Holy Family's household, and in a sketch by Leonardo da Vinci the Christ Child is actually hugging a cat.

Homely cats

From about the 16th century, painters began to portray cats as part of the household, initially as an added element in still-lifes or depictions of peasant interiors. Whereas the right kind of dog could be a status symbol, these cats were humble working animals, and still had a rather low reputation: They appear stealing food, squabbling with dogs or, in Paul de Vos's lively 17th-century *Cat fight in the kitchen,* creating household havoc.

The cat observed

Early feline paintings are stiff and stylized, but by the Renaissance some artists at least were beginning to be fascinated by the fluid curves and elegant poses of cats—as in Leonardo da Vinci's sketches of feline contortions, where they segue into dragons. By the 19th century, painters such as Theophile Steinlen and Henriette Ronner found it worthwhile to specialize in cats as their subjects.

Renoir's cats

By the 19th century, artists had come to appreciate cats as part of the painting's composition. Pierre Auguste Renoir often included cats in his portraits to complement the sitter's pose. In *Woman with a Cat* (c.1875), the young woman cuddles an enchanting tabby kitten, which simultaneously reflects her soft, sweet expression yet adds depth to the portrait by hinting that she too may have hidden claws.

Renoir shows us a cat that is very much at home in the 19th-century drawing room.

Family members

Only recently have individual cats been considered worthy of inclusion in portraits as family members. In 1904–5, publisher Ambrose Voillard, painted with a cat on his lap by Pierre Bonnard, complained that the cat kept him awake during the sittings. More recently, David Hockney's portrait of fashion designer Ossie Clark and his wife with their cat, Percy, has become one of the most popular works in the Tate Gallery.

Hockney's Mr. and Mrs. Clark and Percy. *Celia Birtwell (ex-Mrs. Clark) later claimed that the cat portrayed was, in fact, Blanche, the second cat in the Clark household.*

Picasso's cats

When Pablo Picasso turned his hand to painting cats, he focused on their dark side. His darkly disturbing *Cat Killing a Bird* (1939), painted after the end of the Spanish Civil War, depicts a monstrous predator with a humanized mask of a face and exaggerated claws. Picasso painted a second, even more violent version, which he never sold.

CATS AND MUSIC

Sacred rattle

In ancient Egypt, the cat-headed goddess Bastet was usually portrayed playing a sistrum, a ceremonial rattle, while accompanied by cats or kittens. Her symbols of cat and sistrum were often linked, with sistra decorated with images of cats and sketches depicting animals in human roles that feature the cat itself as the sistrum player.

A bronze statuette of Bastet from c. 664–30 B.C. characteristically shows her with sistrum and kittens.

Feline ballet

The ballet *Les demoiselles de la nuit* ("The ladies of the night"), by French composer Jean Françaix (1912–97), tells the tragic love story of Agathe, a white she-cat who falls in love with a violinist, taking on human form for his sake but ultimately betrayed by her feline nature. At the 1948 premiere, a young Margot Fonteyn, as Agathe, refused to wear her cat mask until the designer swore to set the theater on fire if she didn't.

Music-hall imitations

Victorian music-hall star "Cat" Harris was renowned for his burlesque of Italian opera, in which he imitated cats to the tune of operatic songs. When he was required for a performance at London's Haymarket Theatre, his would-be employers, unable to identify his house, had to locate him by making cat noises outside until he heard and responded "with a cantata of the same sort."

Cats singing

There have been few studies of cats' musical capacity, but 18th-century Italian economist Abbé Ferdinando Galiani claimed to distinguish between tenor and soprano feline voices and to have identified 20 distinct notes in their mews. A century later, French novelist Jules Champfleury capped this by distinguishing 63 separate notes, although he conceded that it took much practice to do so.

Singing, or just yowling? Not many people have found the cat's "song" musical.

Guess what inspired Zez Confrey's popular ragtime piano piece Kitten on the Keys *in 1921!*

Mews as muses

Two classical duets were inspired by nocturnal caterwauling: Rossini's comic *Duetto Buffo di Due Gatti* and a duet in Ravel's opera *L'enfant et les sortileges* with libretto by cat-loving author Colette. Scarlatti's *Cat Fugue* is said to have been inspired by his cats walking on harpsichord keys, Chopin's *Cat Waltz* by a cat playing with a ball of yarn, and Fauré's *Kitty Valse* by a kitten playing.

Music critic

French author Théophile Gautier (1811–72) kept many cats, including a snow-white female named Madam Théophile who had a great taste for music. In his writings he records how when anyone sat at the piano to sing, the white cat would sit among the sheet music listening attentively. However, she objected to high notes, and "she never failed to close the singer's mouth with her paw if the lady sang the high A."

Record-breaking musical

The musical *Cats*, based on T. S. Eliot's comic verse collection *Old Possum's Book of Practical Cats*, seemed an unlikely hit when it opened in 1981, but became the longest-running musical in London and on Broadway. With no spoken dialog, it depicts Eliot's feline characters through dance and song, culminating with Grizabella's performance of the hit song "Memory" before she ascends to feline heaven.

Subtle costumes, makeup, and feline-inspired choreography transformed the cast of Cats.

CATS AND

PEOPLE

CATS AS COMPANIONS

Do cats care?

Cat haters often claim that the relationship between cats and their people is one-sided, viewing cats as selfish opportunists whose apparent affection is all on the surface. Cat lovers, on the other hand, recognize a real bond between themselves and their pets. The truth is that cats, like people, are individuals, with attitudes ranging from total independence to real devotion.

How friendly a cat is depends on many factors, including heredity and kittenhood experiences.

Prison visitor

A devoted 15th-century cat is credited with saving the life of her master, Sir Henry Wyatt. In 1483, Sir Henry was imprisoned by Richard III in the Tower of London, where he would have starved had not a cat befriended him and caught him a pigeon each day for his meal. According to family papers, upon his release from the Tower Sir Henry "would ever make much of cats, as other men will of their spaniels or hounds."

Within these walls

A century later Trixie, a black-and-white cat, displayed a touching devotion to her master, the Earl of Southampton, when he was confined in the Tower of London. Tradition says that, after the Earl's arrest, his cat tracked him across the city and joined him in his cell by climbing down a chimney, remaining with him until he was released. The Earl's portrait shows his faithful cat beside him.

Shortly after his release, the Earl commissioned this portrait by John de Critz the Elder, which includes his faithful cat Trixie.

Child's defender

Godzilla, a fat, lazy tabby living in Idaho, seemed an unlikely hero, but when his owner's five-year-old was savaged by a German shepherd in 1989, it was the cat who shot to his rescue. Godzilla leapt from a tree onto the dog's back and attacked it so fiercely that it dropped its victim and bolted. Doctors who treated the child's injuries were clear that the heroic cat had saved his life.

Alarm bell

In 1977 another Trixie, an Abyssinian from Kansas, came to the rescue when her frail, elderly owner fell outside his home and broke his hip. Nobody heard his cries for help but Trixie, who was equal to the challenge. There

was an old outside dinner bell tied apparently out of her reach, but she made a giant leap and swung on the bell to ring it vigorously, persisting until human help arrived.

Good for people

Research shows that owning cats is good for our health and can increase life expectancy by up to a third. Cat ownership is linked with lower occurrence of high blood pressure and other ills, children born into cat-owning families are less liable to develop asthma, and old people who live alone benefit from feline company—in fact, in parts of the U.S., cats are recommended to elderly people as the best medicine.

Good for cats?

Obviously a cruel or neglectful owner is worse for a cat than no owner at all, but some cat lovers create serious problems. A passion for cats can become the psychological disorder known as cat hoarding. Cat hoarders, with the best intentions, amass more cats than they can cope with (often hundreds), until local authorities or animal rescues have to step in to remove seriously neglected cats from appalling conditions.

Cat rescue

Animal lovers began to set up shelters for stray cats and dogs early in the 19th century, and it was not long before rescue programs specifically for cats were established. Among the first was the London Institution for Lost and Starving Cats, which collected strays in a horse-drawn van and offered free veterinary care to the cats of the poor. Today cats' homes worldwide are still inundated with cats in need.

Many cat rescue programs rely almost entirely on volunteers to look after inmates, raise funds, and carry out errands of mercy.

AILUROPHILES, a.k.a. CAT LOVERS

The Lady with the Lamp

Florence Nightingale (1820–1910), founder of modern nursing, claimed to have learned her philosophy of life from a kitten who refused to back down to an aggressive cat but stood its ground—and kissed the aggressor on the nose. Nightingale owned more than 60 Persian cats over her lifetime, named after great men of the time such as Bismarck and Disraeli, and took them with her wherever she traveled.

The example of Florence Nightingale challenges those who assert that animal lovers have no time for their fellow humans.

Rude Russians

The home of Russian composer Alexander Borodin (1833–87) was dominated by cats who did exactly as they liked—visitors complained of cats on the dinner table "sticking their noses into plates [and] unceremoniously leaping to the diner's back." His favorites included Rybolov ("Fisherman"—named from his favorite hobby) and Dlinyenki ("Long"), who brought home stray kittens to add to the fold.

Poet's pal

Italian poet Petrarch (1304–74), whose poems were inspired by his lost love Laura, found comfort in his cat, "her master's joy in the sunshine, his solace in the shade," and they were not separated in death, for she shares his tomb—a rare honor for a medieval feline. The marble slab where her embalmed body was placed was inscribed with her epitaph: "I was the greatest passion, second only to Laura."

French favorites

French novelist Colette (1873–1954) brought her lifelong passion for cats into her novels. These included *Barks and Purrs,* (*Sept dialogues de bêtes*, 1913), about her gray Angora Kiki-la-Doucette, and *The Cat* (*La Chatte*, 1936), in which the main character, forced to choose between his young bride and his Chartreux cat, Saha, opts for the cat.

It was a dictum of Colette's that "Time spent with cats is never wasted." Here she shares a moment with one of her feline friends, as painted by Jean Texcier.

Hemingway believed cats preferred names with an "s" or "z" sound, so his familiars included Crazy, Ecstasy, and Friendless.

A horrid story

English novelist Thomas Hardy (1840–1928) was inseparable from his beloved Persian cat Cobby, who disappeared mysteriously when Hardy died. However, the macabre tale goes that when Hardy's heart was removed for burial in the local churchyard of Stinsford, Cobby mistook it for dinner. For the benefit of the church ceremony, the undertaker secretly killed the cat and popped him in the casket—after all, Hardy's heart was inside him.

The Hemingway horde

His novels achieved fame, but Ernest Hemingway (1898–1961) also hoped to be remembered for his cats. When living in Cuba (in a house shared by 30-odd pampered felines), he tried to develop his own breed by crossing local cats with Angoras. However, it was the polydactyl (many-toed) cats he kept at his Florida home that perpetuated his name in the feline sense: "Hemingway Cats" descended from his pets are still bred there.

Koko's cats

Humans are not the only pet lovers. Koko the gorilla, born in 1971 and raised to use American sign language, asked her trainer Dr. Penny Paterson (in sign language) in 1984 for a cat of her own. She chose a gray Manx kitten, which she named All Ball and loved dearly. All Ball was run over by a car, and although Koko was consoled by a new cat, Lipstick, when she saw pictures of her first pet years later she would sign "Sad."

Secretarial assistance

Few who read the tough detective thrillers of Raymond Chandler (1888–1959) would imagine that they were written with the assistance of a cat. Chandler called his black Persian Taki his "secretary," for she always attended him while he wrote, sitting on his desk, leaning on his typewriter, or perched on his papers, and listened patiently while he read out his first drafts to her.

SOME DON'T LIKE CATS

Feline phobia

Some people are cat-phobic. They have an irrational but deep-seated fear of cats, leading them to go into a panic state in Puss's presence. This fear is termed "ailurophobia" from the Greek words "ailouros" (cat) and "phobia" (fear). The condition is also, less commonly, called felinophobia or gatophobia. Although cat haters are sometimes described as ailurophobes, this is not strictly correct: being terrified of cats is quite different from detesting them.

Tradition says that Napoleon Bonaparte (left) and Benito Mussolini and Adolf Hitler (right) were cat haters—but were they really?

Dictators and cats

Alexander the Great, Genghis Khan, Julius Caesar, Napoleon Bonaparte, Benito Mussolini, and Adolf Hitler are all said to have loathed cats. In many cases there is no historical evidence that this was the case, but popular tradition insists that dictators and tyrants are portrayed as cat haters whether this be the case or not. Since cats can't be dictated to, they make a perfect emblem to set against dictatorship.

The Sending of Dana Da

Rudyard Kipling's short story *The Sending of Dana Da* (1888), a satire on contemporary occultism, hinges upon ailurophobia. Self-styled mystic Dana Da demonstrates his power by materializing a series of kittens in the home of the ailurophobe, each "in a place where no kitten rightly could or should be." On his deathbed he admits the "gorgeous simplicity" of his plan: he bribed servants to place the kittens.

Kitten on the keys

French author Alphonse Daudet (1840–97) blamed his ailurophobia on a childhood incident when a piano playing itself in an empty room terrified his family. "As if under the gloved fingers of thick mittens, the notes cried feebly at intervals ... as though souls were weeping in the drawing-room." The ghostly pianist was only the family cat, but for the rest of his life cats and terror were linked in Daudet's mind.

An extremist

In the 1920s, cat-hating Chicago banker Rockwell Sayre started a campaign to rid the entire world of cats by the year 1925, offering a financial bounty to cat killers. In the first three months, he reckoned to have had 7 million cats killed. When 1925 came and the cat had not been eradicated, he decided to extend his

The campaign of Rockwell Sayre to rid the world of cats through a policy of deliberate extermination fortunately came to naught.

campaign for a further ten years, but his death soon afterward put an end to his cat war.

Dwight Eisenhower is the only U.S. president known to have hated cats.

Cat persecution

Other active cat haters included dancer Isadora Duncan (1878–1927), who had any cats that wandered into her garden drowned, and U.S. President Dwight D. Eisenhower (1890–1969), who ordered his staff at his Gettysburg home to shoot cats on sight. Tradition says that composer Johannes Brahms (1833–97) liked to shoot cats with a bow and arrow, but this may have been a slander made up by his rival Richard Wagner.

Cats that persecute

Cats seem to gravitate toward ailurophobes, and are always eager to sit on the laps of people who dislike them. This isn't a matter of malevolence but of misinterpretation. Cat lovers often try to attract cats by gesturing, calling, and staring, which in cats' body language is rather rude and offputting. Cat haters, on the other hand, try to deter cats by ignoring them, which is much politer and is taken as an invitation.

In the movies

Ailurophobia inspired *Eye of the Cat*, a 1969 crime thriller movie *(below)*, in which a nephew plotting to murder his wealthy, cat-loving aunt is hampered by his terror of her pets. Before he can tackle his aunt, he has to deal with her swarm of cats. Although the plot hints at some sort of evil intelligence on the part of the cats, the film failed to develop this element and reviewers panned it as a substandard potboiler.

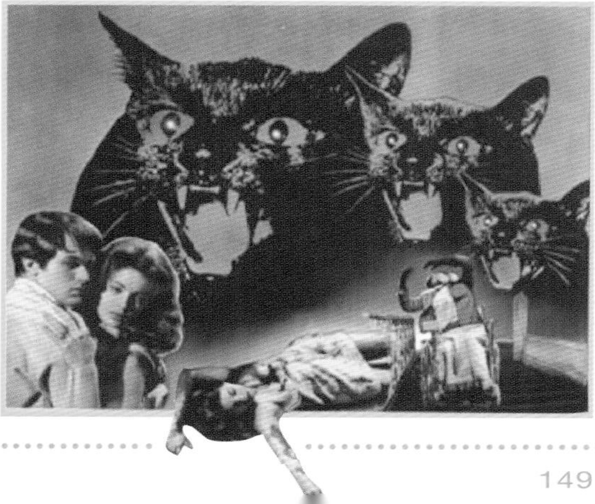

CAT KIT TO BUY

Essentials

Most feline accessories are nonessential. As any cat will tell you, the key item is dinner, so food and water bowls are important—wide, shallow dishes to allow whisker clearance, and ideally ceramic or metal to avoid possible plastic allergies. Where there is input, there will be output, so a litter tray and suitable litter are also vital—not only for indoor cats, but for new arrivals, who should not be allowed out until they feel at home.

Choose food and water bowls with care, and keep them scrupulously clean.

Cat litter

In 1947 American Edward Lowe started a multi-million dollar industry with his accidental invention of cat litter. A neighbor's request for sawdust for her cat's earth tray inspired him to suggest that she try the granulated clay used to soak up spills in his father's workshop. This was so successful that he built up a business and made his fortune selling bags of cat litter.

Cat carrier

A traveling carrier is worth having, even if your cat uses it only to visit the vet for its annual checkup: even the best-behaved cat is simply not safe enough carried in your arms. The carrier needs to be comfortable, well ventilated (but not drafty), escape-proof, and easy to clean, and most cats feel safer in an enclosed box than in a mesh cage that is open on all sides.

Beds

Expensive cat beds may be spurned by pets who prefer to choose their own sleeping places. Comfort matters more to a cat than appearance, and for most so does height—a bed above floor level gives a feeling of security. Many cats elect to roost in places that look most uncomfortable to us. However, a cozy bed placed in a site of the cat's choosing is often more than acceptable.

An imaginative range of interactive toys is available to give Puss hours of amusement.

Toys

Cats often remain playful well into old age, and they do enjoy their toys—and their owners often get as much pleasure as they give in providing a variety of playthings. Different cats like different toys—cuddly, rattly, or squeaky. "Fishing-rod" toys that can be dangled are a

▲ *Check your cat's collar regularly to be sure it is comfortable and still a good fit.*

great favorite and also keep your fingers out of the way of claws.

Cat doors

For outdoor cats, investing in a cat door *(right)* will spare you doorman duty. Doors that are lockable from either side allow you the option of shutting your cat in or out, and ones that are operated by a magnet on the cat's collar will keep out feline trespassers. Isaac Newton is said to have invented the cat door when he cut a hole in his own door for his cat's use—and then cut another smaller door for her kittens!

Collars

A collar is a must for a dog, but an optional extra for a cat. Few cats enjoy walking on a lead, and those who do are safest in a harness. If you plan to take an indoor cat out on a lead for fresh air, get him used to it inside first. For free-ranging cats, a collar with address tag can be valuable as a means of identification, although it must be a safety collar with an elastic or quick-release section in case it catches on a branch.

Scratching posts

These are appreciated by most cats, and essential for indoor pets with no access to trees for claw care. Some cats won't see the point of scratching posts *(right)* so long as there are chair legs available, but if you value your furniture, you must provide an alternative—and encourage its use. Rubbing the post with catnip or using an attractant spray available from pet shops often does the trick.

Cat furniture

Pet stores supply an astonishing range of climbing frames for cats, some quite elaborate with perches, hidey-holes, and scratching posts. Although outdoor cats have a world of trees and rooftops to explore, such cat furniture can be very beneficial to indoor cats, providing a more stimulating environment and encouraging healthy exercise.

CAT KIT TO MAKE

Simple scratching post

A coir doormat firmly attached to an upright wall provides everything a cat wants in a scratching post. To encourage your pet to make use of it, rub catnip on it to create an inviting smell.

Hide-and-seek toys

Throw-away packaging makes great cat toys—for free. Most cats love hidey-holes to play in, so a simple cardboard box with a hole cut in one side will provide a cat with hours of amusement, as will a large, rustly paper bag. Your cat will soon look forward with pleasure to your return from a shopping expedition.

Most cats just love a paper bag—a hidey-hole with built-in amusing sound effects.

Cheap and cheerful

Wadded-up tinfoil makes a great "ball" for a cat to play with. Lightweight enough for a paw to bat about, it is also easily carried and has the bonus of making fascinating rustly noises. A basic soft toy for hunting games can be made by stuffing a child's sock with catnip and stitching or tying off the end securely. Cats also love rattly mobiles: try hanging up a chain of linked plastic shower-curtain rings.

Whether playing alone or with a human friend, dangly toys are perennial favorites.

Upwardly mobile

Few cats can resist a dangling mobile, and it's easy to attach a few items to a length of elastic and hang it up within your pet's reach. Alternating different types of mobile will keep his interest. Try a "soft toy" version with woolly pompoms and scraps of fur fabric, and a "rattle" type with seashells, pinecones, plastic shower-curtain rings, and the like. Feathers are always popular, and small bells add to the fun.

Winter warmer

Materials:
- Two 6-in. (15-cm) squares of lightweight cotton fabric
- Sewing thread
- Small bag of bran or oatmeal
- Teaspoonful of dried lavender

Method:
Lay the fabric squares on top of each other (**1**) and stitch them together along three sides (**2**), leaving a 0.25-in. (6-mm) border. Stitch part of each end of the fourth side, leaving a gap in the center. Turn inside out to form a bag, and stuff loosely with the bran or oatmeal and lavender before stitching shut the opening (**3**). Warm the bag in the microwave for 1–2 minutes until it is pleasantly warm (but not too hot) and place in your cat's bed, to provide a safe alternative to a hot-water bottle.

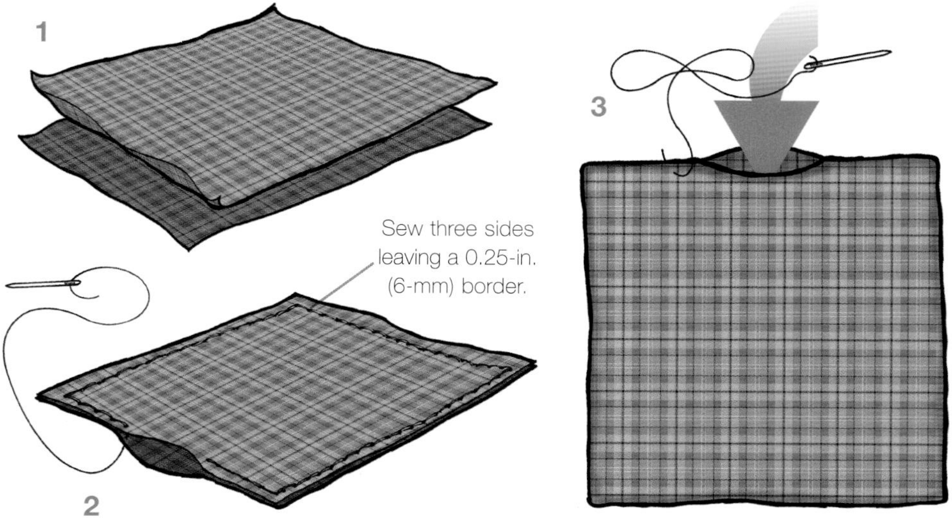
1
Sew three sides leaving a 0.25-in. (6-mm) border.
2
3

SPOILED CATS

Moving expenses

Artist and master of nonsense verse Edward Lear (1812–88) dearly loved his cat Foss, an enormous, dock-tailed tabby. In fact, when he moved to a new house, he instructed his architect to build an exact reproduction of his own home so that Foss's routine would not be disturbed. When Foss died, in 1887, he was buried under a large tombstone in Lear's Italian garden, and his master did not long survive him.

Edward Lear's drawing of the rotund cat on which he doted—"my poor friend Foss."

Rich cats

In the early 1960s, 15-year-old Hellcat and Brownie of San Diego became the richest cats in the world when their owner left them nearly $415,000. In 1986 a British cat, 12-year-old Minky, inherited a mere £10,000 "to keep her in style for the rest of her life"—enough to provide a daily menu ranging from poached cod in parsley sauce to chicken served with a side portion of chopped livers.

The cardinal's cats

At a time when cats were generally associated with witchcraft and persecuted, Cardinal Richelieu (1585–1642) kept and adored no fewer than 14 felines, reserving the room next to his own for their use and employing two servants to feed them chicken pâté twice a day. He also provided for the cats and their caretakers in his will.

A helping hand

Visitors to the famous African clinic of Nobel Prize–winning missionary-doctor Albert Schweitzer (1875–1965) noted his deep affection for his cat Sizi and the way he pandered to her every need. Sizi liked to sleep across her master's arm, preventing him from working. Rather than disturb her, he taught himself to write with his other hand, becoming completely ambidextrous in her service.

Albert Schweitzer taught himself to write with either hand to avoid disturbing Sizi.

Cats' Café

The world's first restaurant opened exclusively for cats to dine with their owners, the Meow Mix Cafe opened on Manhattan's Fifth Avenue, New York, in August 2004. Opened for just five days, but with a proposal to reopen permanently at a later date, the restaurant provided a menu offering feline customers a choice of six different flavors of cat food, and had only two rules: no dogs and no catnip.

A statue to Dr. Johnson's Hodge now stands in Gough Square in London, where he once lived.

A very fine cat indeed

Writer and lexicographer Dr. Samuel Johnson (1709–84) could be acerbic with mere humans, but was positively indulgent toward his "very fine cat" Hodge. Hodge had a taste for oysters, and Johnson would go out to buy these himself rather than bother the servants, for fear that they might 'take a dislike to the poor creature" if they had to run errands for a cat.

Safe harbor

The 60 cats who reside on De Poezenboot ("the Pussycat Boat"), a barge moored alongside Singel Canal in Amsterdam, deserve to be spoiled more than most. Since 1969 the barge, now a notable tourist attraction, has been a home for Amsterdam's stray cats, and is now reserved as a residence for cats too old or ill to be rehomed. A second boat accommodates young, healthy cats awaiting homes.

Kitty treats

Today you can buy your pet elaborate cat furniture, designer collars, and even DVDs and videos made especially to entertain cats. Those who want the ultimate in togetherness can even purchase a Japanese two-seater toilet whose second, smaller seat is designed for feline use, complete with a fish-shaped ring to allow the cat to flush after use.

Every cat admitted to the care of De Poezenboot in Amsterdam is neutered to counteract the serious problem of strays.

DIET

No vegetarian option

Cats are not vegetarians, or even omnivores. They are carnivores with a higher protein requirement than most mammals—in proportion to size, more than double that of dogs or humans—and they need a meat diet. Meat contains essential amino acids that cats cannot synthesize themselves, a deficiency in which carries a high risk of serious and irreversible damage to the cat's heart and eyes.

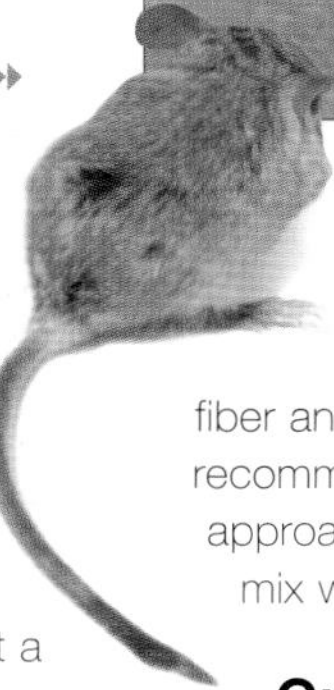

Mice contain all the nutrients a cat needs—but also carry the risk of parasites.

Little and often

One large meal a day doesn't suit cats nearly as well as a series of small ones. In the wild, they would live on small prey like mice, caught at intervals throughout the day, rather than gorging themselves to satiation at one time like lions. It takes the equivalent of about ten mice per day to meet a cat's food requirements, and a natural eating pattern would be up to 16 small meals over 24 hours.

Commercial diets

Most pet cats don't need to hunt for food, but rely on us to provide their meals. Canned, dried, and semi-moist cat foods are scientifically designed to meet their dietary needs. A raw-food diet made up of 75–80 percent meat, with pulped or grated vegetables or grains for fiber and bonemeal for calcium, is also often recommended, although novices to this approach should research the appropriate mix with care.

Commercial foods also provide a balanced diet, and come in a range of shapes and flavors.

Greens and grains

Cats don't need carbohydrates at all, as they derive most of their energy from proteins, but they can make use of carbohydrates if these form part of their diet, so a limited amount of cooked grains or potatoes is acceptable. They do need some vegetables, such as carrots, zucchini, pumpkin, or cooked sweet potatoes, as these provide valuable fiber and help to prevent fur balls and constipation.

Grow a salad pot

Outdoor cats are often seen nibbling at grass in the garden, probably for its fiber content. Indoor cats can be offered the same facilities with grass grown in a pot—most pet stores stock prepackaged "cat grass" seeds of suitable varieties. Once the grass is a couple of inches long, it can be made available for chewing at regular intervals, and may deflect a cat's attention from favored indoor plants.

Indoor grass pots are a safer option than outdoor lawns, which may be contaminated with chemicals.

Obesity

Most cats regulate their own food intake, and obesity is less common than in dogs. However, some individuals manage to put on too much weight, and studies suggest that non-pedigree cats, males, neuters, and indoor cats are most at risk. Fat cats are not healthy cats, and need to be encouraged to lose weight gradually by reducing calorie intake and increasing activity—playtime helps cats to slim!

Say no to milk

A saucer of milk for the cat is a traditional treat, but today we know that many adult cats are actually allergic to cows' milk, which causes them upset stomachs. Oddly enough, cream is usually safer than milk, as it contains less lactose than whole or skim milk. For milk-loving cats who can't digest their favorite, lactose-free milk substitutes specially designed for cats can be bought at most pet stores.

Hazardous foods

Chocolate is toxic to cats, dark chocolate being the most dangerous. As little as 16 oz. (450 g) can be a fatal dose for a feline. Although cats don't have a sweet tooth, some find chocolate very attractive, so keep this treat well out of their reach. Other foodstuffs to avoid include onions, garlic, raisins, grapes, tomatoes, and raw potatoes, all of which can cause serious health problems.

Letting your cats share a dish means you have no control over who eats what. You may end up with one fat cat and one thin one.

COOKING FOR CATS

Main Courses

Scrambled egg

1 egg, lightly beaten with a little water
1 teaspoon finely chopped fresh parsley
1 teaspoon finely chopped cabbage
1 oz./25 g dry cat food
1 teaspoon butter
Melt the butter in a small pan, pour in the egg, and whisk until lightly scrambled. Remove pan from heat, stir in the other ingredients, and allow to cool before serving.

Kipper delight

4 oz./100 g cooked kipper
3 oz./75 g cooked carrots
2 eggs
2 oz./50 g grated cheese
Milk to mix
Mash together fish and vegetables and put the mixture into a greased baking pan. Beat the eggs, milk, and cheese together and pour on top of the fish mixture. Bake at 325° F/165° C for 20 minutes until set. Allow to cool before serving.

Until World War II, British cats looked forward to the visits of the cats' meat man, who sold meat unfit for human consumption—and sometimes too ripe for cats as well.

Liver and kidney

1 chicken liver, finely chopped
½ lamb's kidney, finely chopped
1 small piece unsmoked bacon, de-rinded and chopped
1 baby carrot, cooked
1 tablespoon oatmeal
Cook the meat in boiling water for 3 minutes; drain and mash with the remaining ingredients. Serve slightly warm for maximum appeal.

Snacks

Yeasty crunchies

Whole wheat bread crusts
Yeast extract, dissolved in hot water
Cut the crusts into bite-sized pieces and spread lightly with the yeast extract. Spread them on a baking sheet and bake at 275° F/135° C on the lowest shelf of the oven until crisp. Cool and store in an airtight container.

Most cats love sardines, but they will love them even more in a cream cheese and watercress sandwich.

Sardine sandwiches

Can of sardines in oil
Cream cheese
Finely chopped watercress
Whole-wheat bread
Drain the sardines, then mash the first three ingredients till smooth. Make sandwiches with the bread, and cut into bite-sized pieces.

Sausage squares

3 oz./75 g sausage meat
2 tablespoons oatmeal
1 egg
1 teaspoon chopped parsley
Mix all the ingredients together and form into a flat cake. Grill under medium heat for about 5 minutes until the outside is crisp. Allow to cool, then cut into small pieces.

THE CAT-FRIENDLY GARDEN

Sharing space

What a cat likes in a garden is somewhere to sit in the sun, somewhere to sit in the shade, earth to dig in, plants that smell good, hiding places, and the odd high perch. What a gardener doesn't like in a cat is indiscriminate toileting and digging up of flower beds, problems that can be minimized by allocating a private corner of the garden especially for feline use.

Cats love finding shady corners in a garden where they can retreat from the world and keep an eye open for any unsuspecting bird or small rodent that may just cross their path.

Shady shelters

Cats appreciate having somewhere to shelter from prying eyes and also from sun and rain. Lurking under a bush may satisfy this need, but you can also provide one or more purpose-built refuges. Store-bought plastic shelters are waterproof and durable, or, for simplicity, you can simply make a small tepee of boards. Tuck the shelter away in the shrubbery or paint and shingle it as a decorative garden feature.

Kitty corner

Pick a corner at the back of the garden to give your cat privacy. At the back, place a sandbox—a wooden frame (at least two cats long and one cat wide) set on the earth and filled with 4–6 in. (15–20 cm) of sand, which can be cleaned easily. (Bare earth as an "outdoor litter tray" quickly becomes fouled and impacted.) Add cat-attractant plants (see below), with tall plants at the front to provide a screen.

Wildlife protection

Garden birds are vulnerable to cat predation. If you have bird feeders, position them high out of your cat's reach; hanging bird-tables are safer than the traditional freestanding variety (which

Adopting organic gardening principles is a good way to make your garden cat friendly; avoiding chemicals and pesticides ensures a safe environment for cats.

Feline Favorites		
Plant	**Conditions**	**Appearance**
Catnip *(Nepeta cataria)*	Full sun in well-drained soil	Height 9–12 in. (23–30 cm). Tiny lavender flowers.
Catmint *(Nepeta mussinii)*	Full sun or partial shade	Height 18–24 in. (46–60 cm). Silvery leaves, white to dark blue flowers.
Cat thyme *(Teucrium marum)*	Full sun in moist, well-drained spot	Height 18–24 in. (46–60 cm). With deep green leaves, purple flower spires.
Valerian *(Valeriana officinalis)*	Sun or partial shade; most soils	Height 3–4 ft. (90–120 cm). Fernlike foliage, pink, white or lavender flowers.
Heather *(Calluna* or *Erica* spp.*)*	Sun. *Calluna*—acid soil; *Erica*—lime tolerant	Range of heights. Various shades of purple or white flowers.
Prostrate rosemary *(Rosmarinus officinalis prostratus)*	Full sun in well-drained soil	Height 1–3 ft. (30–90 cm). Fragrant blue flowers.
Thyme *(Thymus* spp.*)*	Full sun in well-drained soil	Height 6–12 in. (15–30 cm). Pink or mauve flowers.
Alyssum *(Lobularia maritima)*	Full or partial sun; most soils	Height 6–9 in. (15–23 cm). White or pink flowers.
Grass	Sun or shade; most soils	Most cats like to nibble grass, so leave an unmown area for an occasional buffet.

many cats view as restaurant seats). Ponds are fun for cats to watch, but you may need netting to protect fish, frogs, and newts.

Plant protection

Commercial cat repellents can be useful to protect particular areas or plants. Safe and effective homemade deterrents include tea leaves, orange peel, or, for acid-loving plants, diluted vinegar; mothballs are also effective, but dangerous: use them only inside a can with holes in the lid to safeguard your cat. Shield vulnerable plants by laying prickly twigs on the soil beneath them.

Cat protection

Cats have too much sense to eat poisonous plants, so although many plants may be classed as potentially dangerous, this is not a real worry. Garden chemicals, from fertilizers to weedkillers, are much more of a risk, and must be kept securely out of reach.

CAT COLLECTIBLES

Postage stamps

Stamps featuring cats must be among the most attractive of small and affordable cat collectibles. Thousands of different cat stamps have appeared since the first was issued in 1877 in Germany, featuring a cat with a fish in its mouth. Ranging from fine art to photographs, and from breed studies to cartoon cats, there is a wide enough selection to delight any cat lover.

The world is your oyster when it comes to collecting postage stamps with a feline theme.

Carousel cats

For those who prefer larger and scarcer collectibles, what about antique wooden carousel animals? Cats are among the rarest animals to be found among these spectacular examples of folk art, but two American

These fine cats ride the Dentzel Carousel at Castle Amusement Park, Riverside, CA.

companies (Hersell-Spilman and the Dentzel Carousel Works) created some wonderful carousel cats, in particular the playful felines of Dentzel craftsman Salvatore Cerniglario.

Cuddly kitties

Vintage stuffed toys are rare, most having been literally loved to pieces by their young owners, but today's toys are tomorrow's collectibles. The famous German firm Steiff has been producing cats as soft toys since the early 1900s. Their very rare, and very expensive, early models are appealingly naïve; their modern range includes such fashionable breeds as the Balinese, Maine Coon, and British Blue.

Catty containers

Since 1869, when a Cadbury's chocolate box featured a child clutching a tabby cat, cats have adorned tins and boxes containing anything from soap to cigarettes and from cookies to metal polish. Many of the early tins were attractive enough to be preserved after the contents had been used, and are still valued today, such as the cat-shaped candy tins popular in the U.S. between 1890 and 1930.

The legacy of famous glassmaker René Lalique endures in these contemporary crystal cats.

China and pottery

Ceramic cats come in a range to suit every taste and every pocket, from rare Chinese porcelain via later, more affordable models all the way to kitty kitsch. Some of the most treasured are famous 18th-century makes such as Meissen, Chelsea, Delft, and Derby. More accessible are German fairings of the late 1800s and early 1900s, and early-20th-century English souvenir cats decorated with local coats-of-arms.

Glassware

Among the easiest items to find in this field are simple blown-glass cats in quirky shapes and colors, cat-shaped glass perfume bottles, and stained-glass window hangers. More famous are the glass cats of art nouveau designers such as René Lalique, the Daum brothers, and Emil Gallé. Fifty years after Lalique's death, his classic crouching cat in frosted lead crystal is still in production.

Tony Wood Studio cat teapots are much sought-after modern collectibles.

This polished stone cat figurine is obviously influenced by Ancient Egyptian statues of Bastet.

CAT COLLECTIBLES

Metalware

Metal cats can be found in the forms of cast-iron money boxes, doorstops, toasting forks, bottle openers, and even bird scarers, as well as more naturalistic statuettes. One famous range is the Austrian bronzes made between 1880 and 1920, depicting miniature costumed cats as musicians, skaters, billiards players, and carrying out various feline occupations.

An unusual door knocker in the form of a cat's head gripping a ring in its jaws. Some modern knockers even feature different cat breeds.

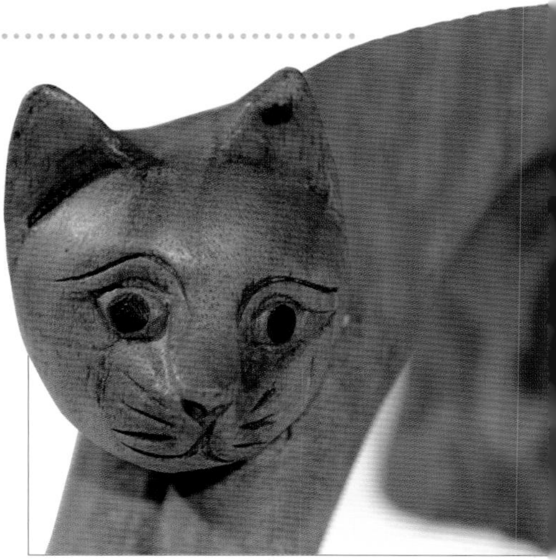

Modern wooden cats are widely available, often carved in a charmingly naïve style and either brightly painted or in natural wood.

Wood carvings

Some of the most enchanting carved cats are Japanese netsuke, miniature masterpieces both old and modern. Then there are the 19th-century carved wooden cats popular with collectors, including German toys and the popular spotted cats favored by Pennsylvania woodcarvers. Today carved cats are produced all over the world, naturalistic, stylized, rustic, comical, and eminently collectible.

Postcards

Picture postcards were invented in 1870, although at first one side was reserved for the address and senders had to squeeze in their message around the picture on the other side. In 1902 the postcard really took off, following the bright idea of dividing the space on the back of the card to accommodate both message and address. Since then the range of cat postcards has been endless!

Cat jewelry

Cats have inspired an incredible range of jewelry—brooches, earrings, pins, and pendants in every material from gold to plastic and in every style from the elegant to the tacky. Some modern jewelers produce meticulously detailed gold or silver cats, at rest or engaged in play in enchantingly realistic attitudes, and there are also delightful ranges in pewter for budget buyers.

Needlework cats

Collectors are unlikely to find anything as old as the cat embroidered by Mary Queen of Scots on her bed hangings in the 16th century. However, the 19th-century craze for Berlin woolwork produced many appealing needlepoint cats (most sought-after being those in velvet-textured plush stitch). Several modern designers have produced charts to enable modern stitchers to produce similar pieces.

The scrapbooking revival has led to the reissue of fun "scraps" like this.

Paper ephemera

The 19th century saw a plethora of printed and embossed paper "scraps" for scrapbooks, which include cats and kittens galore. Other collectable feline ephemera include advertisements, trade and cigarette cards, calendars, Christmas and birthday cards, and posters by such notable artists as Louis Wain, Théophile-Alexandre Steinlen, and John Hassall.

Elegant, stylized, or downright comical cats make delightful small garden ornaments.

A popular Victorian subject for needlepoint, re-created by Elizabeth Bradley.

AN ORIGAMI CAT—MAKING THE HEAD

Origami is the Japanese art of folding paper to make cleverly shaped models, such as flowers, birds, or animals. This cute cat creation is made of two separate sections. No scissors or glue needed—just careful, accurate folds.

1 Begin with a square of paper. Make a crease diagonally across the horizontal centerline from corner to corner, then open the paper out flat again. Now fold the top corner down to meet the centerline, and fold the bottom corner underneath to about half the depth of the lower triangular section.

2 Fold the top half of the paper downward along the line of the centerline fold.

3 Establish the vertical centerline of the model and then fold down the top left and right corners so that their edges meet along this vertical line. The shape you should see will be a small square set on its point like a diamond.

4 Now fold up the bottom two "wings" obliquely so that their tips project over the top sides of the square. These will form the cat's ears.

5 Fold down the top triangular section of the head so that its sides align with the two sloping edges of the ears that you have just made.

6 Turn the whole origami head over. Now fold down just the tip of the triangular section of paper that you see at the bottom of the model. This makes the cat's nose.

7 Here is the finished head. It just needs you to draw some eyes, whiskers, and a mouth for a real feline charmer to emerge!

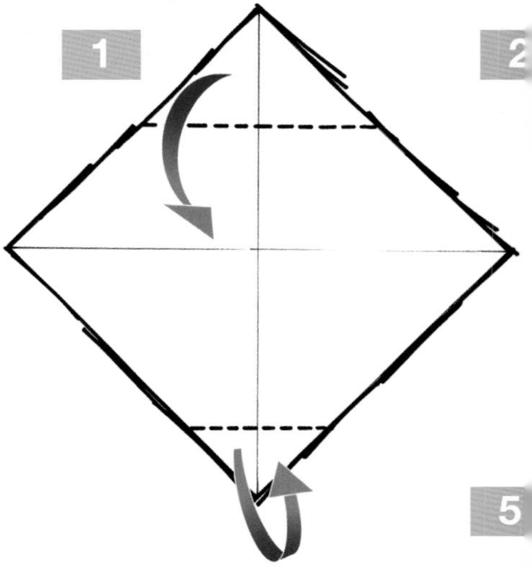

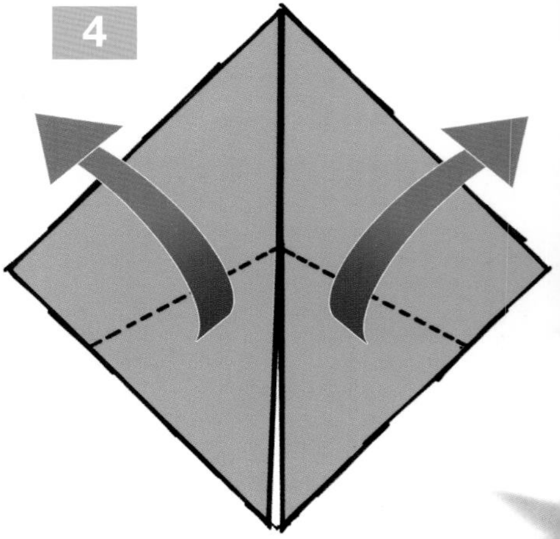

Why not...

use differently colored papers to create an entire family of fun cats? Single colors, tiger stripes, leopard spots, psychedelic flower power—the choice is yours.

For instructions on how to make the cat's body, see overleaf.

AN ORIGAMI CAT—MAKING THE BODY

The cat's body is quite straightforward to make. Some of the folds require a little dexterity as you squash down to flatten out the tail section and then fold it back on itself (Steps **5**, **6**, and **7**), but practice makes perfect.

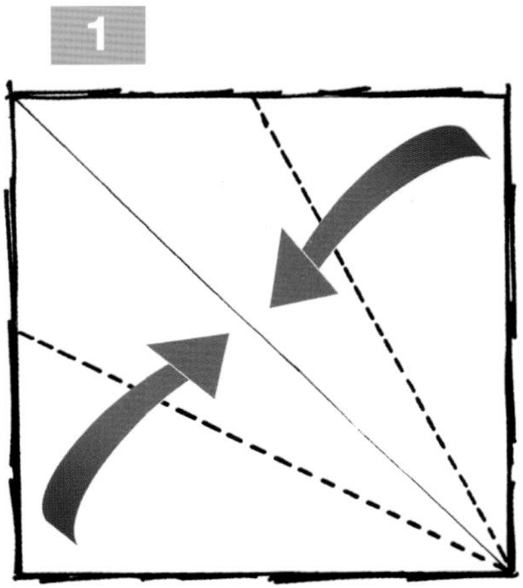

1 Again start with a square of paper and fold in the top and bottom corners so that their edges meet along the diagonal centerline of the paper.

2 Your model should now be kite-shaped. Fold it in half along the diagonal centerline.

3 Fold the right-hand corner of the model downward so that the pointed end is now facing toward you.

4 The next stage is a little tricky. You have to insert your right forefinger inside the little pocket shape that has been made and roll it backward…

5 … while at the same time pressing down and flattening out the resulting kite shape with your left hand. Press in these folds securely so that the model lies flat.

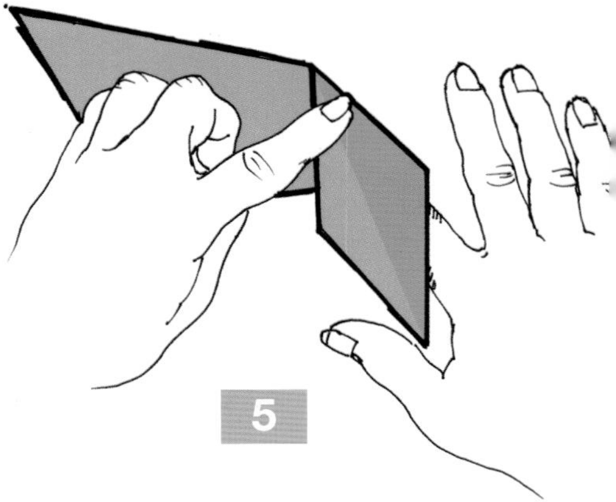

6 Fold up the lower section of the kite shape so that its baseline aligns with the bottom of tł whole body section.

7 Now fold the entire tail section that you have made in half. If you press on the lower corner as you do this, the body section will flap over to enclose the tail neatly.

8 Turn the completed body over and slide the head over the point at the front. You've done it—the origami cat is finished!

Folding tips

Part of the secret of successful origami lies in making sure that the folds are securely creased. Take care with your paper alignment and then use a fingernail to score the fold accurately. This should keep the paper from "bouncing back."

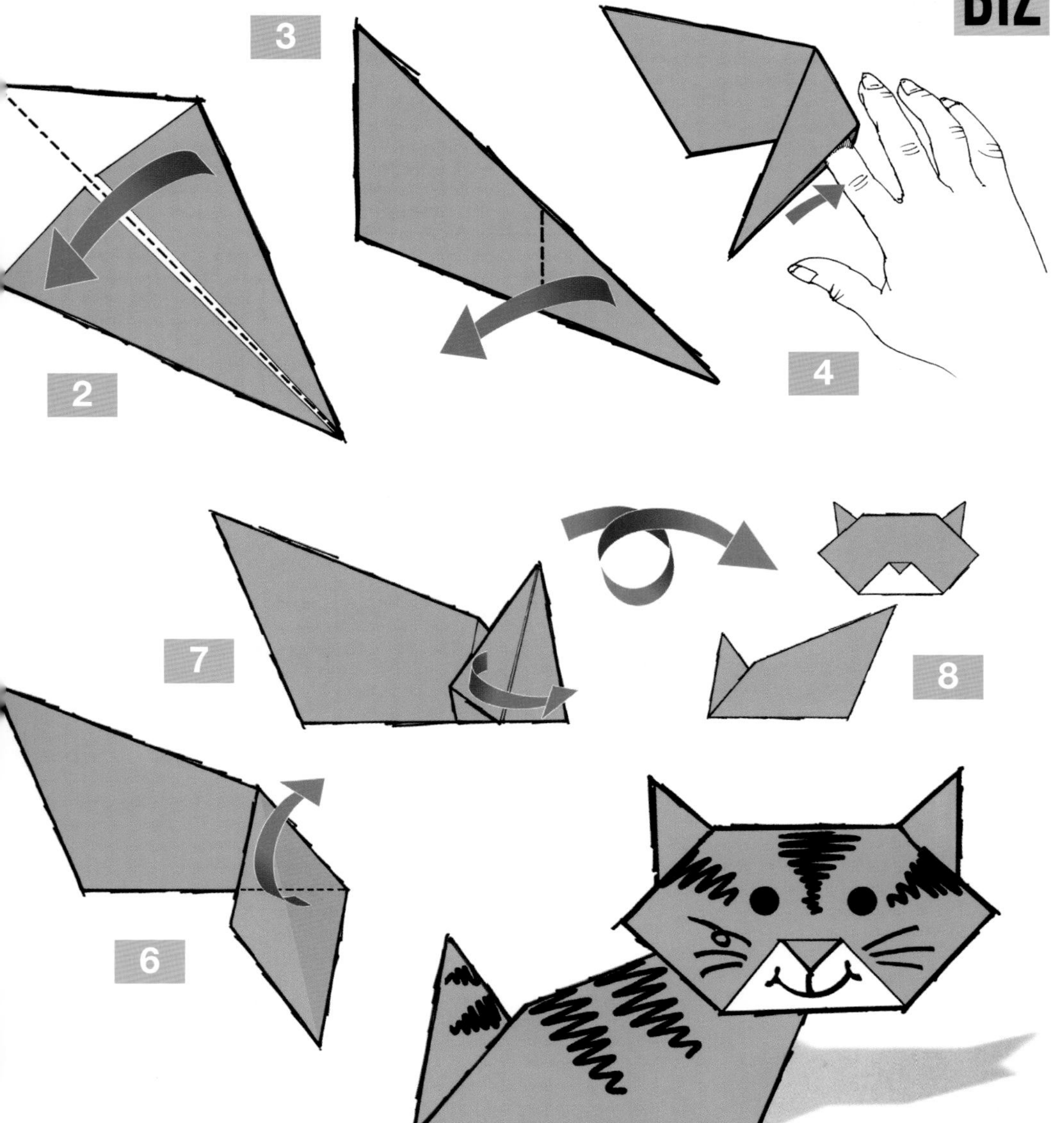

2
3
4
6
7
8

TOPIARY CATS

For all those cat lovers who also enjoy gardening and the pleasures of horticulture, what could be more rewarding than creating a piece of living art in the form of a topiary cat? Today it is possible to buy ready-made wire frames from specialty manufacturers or from garden centers that relieve the prospective topiarist of the burden of constructing the underlying frame. They are available in a wide variety of animal shapes, including a number of alluring cats. These can be cultivated in different ways, as described below.

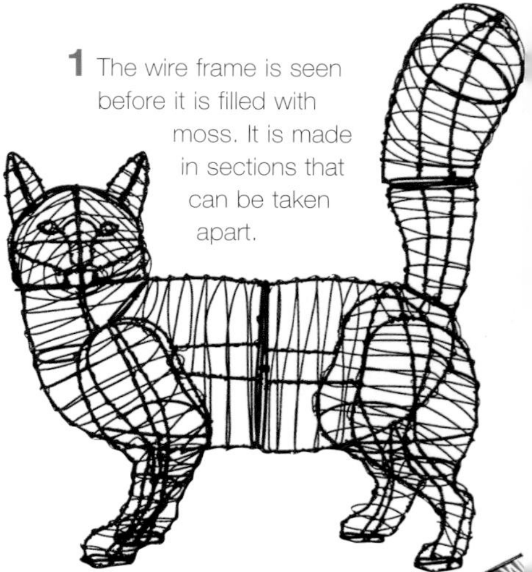

1 The wire frame is seen before it is filled with moss. It is made in sections that can be taken apart.

Planting from outside the form

For this method the frame is filled with sphagnum moss as a suitable growing medium. The moss-filled form is soaked in water and allowed to drain. Then small plant "plugs" are inserted through gaps in the wire frame and planted directly into the moss. Once the frame is fully planted, it should be watered with a good starter fertilizer and kept in a shaded area out of the wind for a few days to let the plants get established before moving it to the chosen area of the garden for display. This style of topiary needs regular watering and fertilization, much as you would a hanging basket.

Water before adding plants.

The moss should be well soaked.

In-ground planting

This more traditional style of topiary calls for plants that are rooted in the soil to be grown into the shape of the cat frame. This can either be achieved by positioning the frame over a plant like a box bush and allowing it to grow into the shape of the form, or by training fast-growing plants such as ivy to grow over the exterior of the frame and so adopt its shape. In both cases the topiary plants will need to be clipped to shape regularly once they are established.

1 Here ivy is being trained to grow up the legs of the frame.

2 Once the frame has been filled with moss, it is ready for planting.

It pays to think about the texture that you want to create with foliage before making the final selection of plants to use. Rockery-type plants that are low growing and invasive make excellent subjects for topiary. It also makes sense to use plants that thrive in the same growing conditions.

2 The growing plants are tied into the frame.

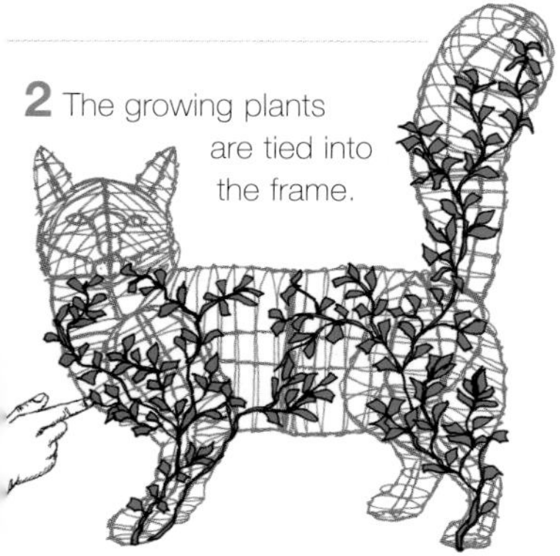

3 Regular clipping helps to establish the shape.

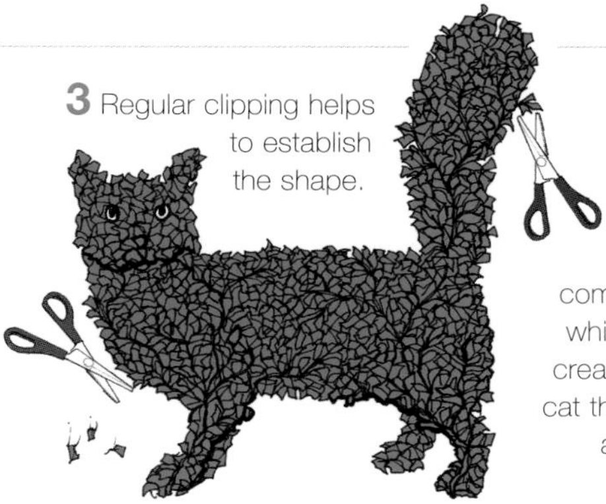

Adding detail like eyes (available commercially) and whiskers helps to create a convincing cat that is fit to grace any garden.

A PAPIER-MÂCHÉ CAT

You will need:
Empty plastic bottle
Bubble wrap
Wallpaper paste
Newspaper
Nonshiny adhesive tape
Cardboard for ears

1 Scrunch bubble wrap into a roughly triangular shape and tape it to the bottle.

2 Wad up bubble wrap into a ball and secure this to the top of the bottle to form a head.

3 Tear newspaper into narrow strips. One at a time, apply paste to the strips and cover the basic shape with overlapping strips, laying alternate layers horizontally and vertically.

4 On the opposite side from the body section, add rolls of bubble wrap to build up the shape of forelegs and front paws. Then cover the legs and paws with more strips of paper to create a smooth finish.

5 Use strips to mold the head into a feline shape. Cut ears out of cardboard and attach with more paper strips, building up the back of the ears more thickly.

Use a thin roll of bubble wrap to form a tail, and attach this to the body with more paper strips.

Allow to dry for a week or so before painting.

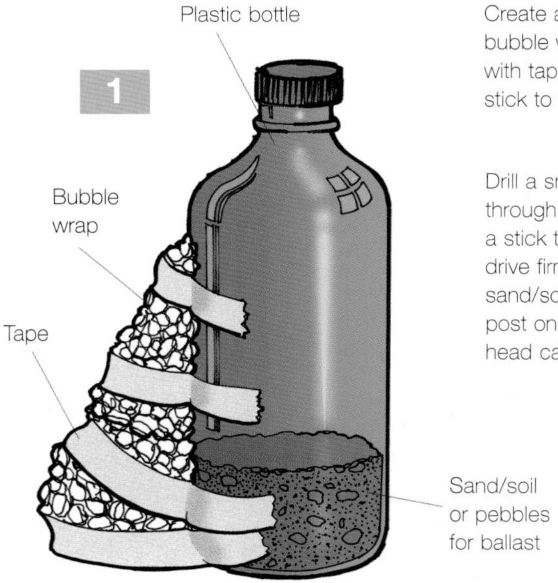
1
Plastic bottle
Bubble wrap
Tape
Sand/soil or pebbles for ballast

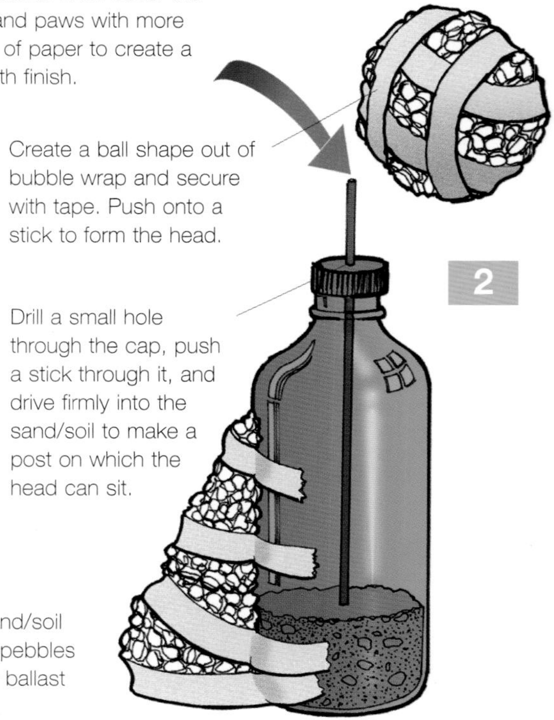
2
Create a ball shape out of bubble wrap and secure with tape. Push onto a stick to form the head.
Drill a small hole through the cap, push a stick through it, and drive firmly into the sand/soil to make a post on which the head can sit.

3

Cover the bottle and head with paper strips to build up the shape of the cat.

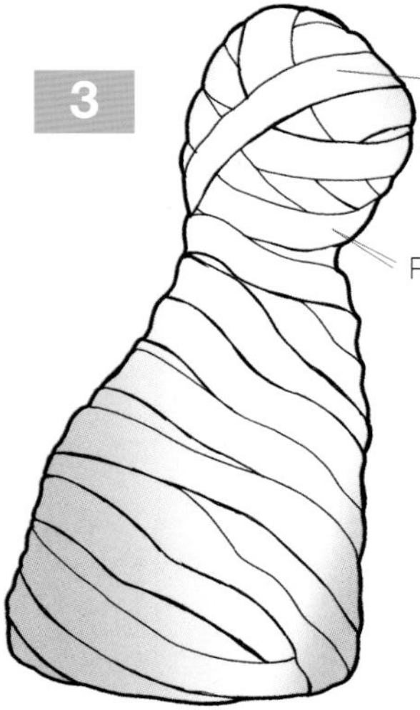

After step 3 is completed, allow the paper strips to dry thoroughly.

Cut the ears from thick cardboard and attach to the head.

Paint the cat in the color of your choice. Allow the paint to dry.

4

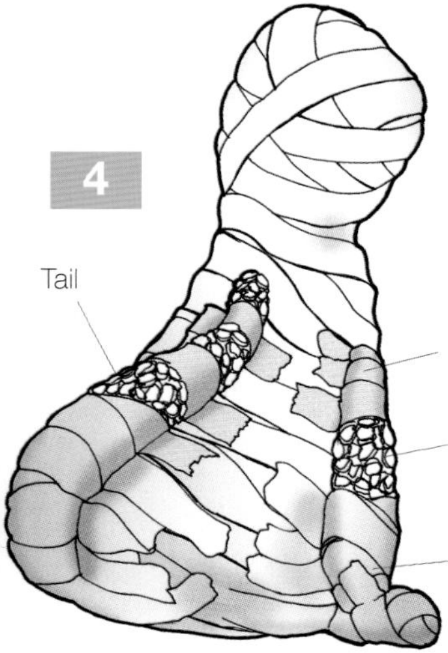

5

Finally, use a marker to draw in ears, eyes, nose, mouth, whiskers, and claws.

CAT CARE—TOP TIPS

Vaccination

Vaccination against common killer diseases such as cat flu and feline enteritis is essential, along with regular boosters, particularly for outdoor cats. Indoor cats won't be exposed to as much risk from disease, but it is perfectly possible for human visitors to carry in infection unknowingly, so play it safe. Worming and flea treatment also need to be carried out regularly.

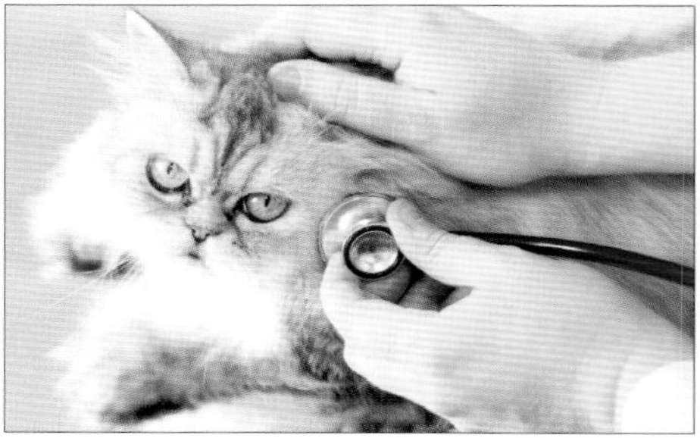

The annual booster vaccination provides the opportunity for a full veterinary checkup.

Neutering

Neutering not only prevents cats from contributing to feline population problems but makes their lives safe—and longer. Neutered cats don't roam as widely, are less exposed to infections and fights, and don't run the risk of reproductive disorders such as uterine infections or prostate problems. Neutering also reduces behavioral problems like urine marking.

Spaying leaves only a tiny flank scar, with an area of shaved fur that will quickly regrow.

Safety first

Don't let curiosity kill your cat! Cat-proofing your home can save your pet's life. Put away household chemicals such as detergents and bleach, along with medicines and small objects such as elastic bands and paper clips that can be swallowed. Secure electrical wires so that a cat can't play with them or chew them, and watch out for open upstairs windows through which your pet might jump.

Hygiene matters

Litter trays *(below)* need to be kept clean, not only to maintain human standards of hygiene but for your cat's comfort. Cats don't like soiled facilities, and may well make a dirty protest if faced with them. Wash the tray with mild soap—the smell of strong detergents is as off-putting to a cat as total squalor.

HEALTH—WARNING SIGNS		
Symptoms	**Common Causes**	**Action**
Scratching, excess licking	Parasites; allergies; wounds	Check skin for flea droppings (apply flea spray) or wounds (may need veterinary attention).
Shaking head and scratching ears	Ear mites; ear infection	Check ears for dark, gritty wax (apply mite medication) or inflammation (see vet—never neglect infections).
Bad breath and drooling	Gum infection	See vet. Reduce risk in future by providing bones/hard cat biscuits to help clean teeth.
Runny nose and sneezing	Viral or bacterial infection; allergy; foreign body in nose	See vet. Prevent infections by vaccination. Allergies may respond to treatment. Foreign bodies not uncommon.
Runny or inflamed eyes	Viral or bacterial infection; injury	See vet. Prevent infections by vaccination. Never neglect eye injuries.
Coughing	Upper respiratory/ chest infection; allergy; heart disease	Never ignore: see vet for diagnosis.
Vomiting	Grass eating; hairballs; may indicate more serious metabolic disorder	See vet if persistent. Occasional vomiting after eating grass not a problem. Prevent hairballs by grooming and attention to diet.
Diarrhea or constipation	Dietary problems; parasites; infections; digestive disorder	See vet if persistent. Diarrhea may respond to a short fast.
Weight loss	Kidney or thyroid problems, especially in older cats	If cat is eating normally but still losing weight, see vet for a full investigation.
Wheezing	Viral or bacterial infection; allergy; chest or diaphragm injury	See vet immediately: breathing problems should never be taken lightly.

THE CAT IN OLD AGE

How old is old?

Cats vary as much as humans when it comes to aging. The average feline lifespan is usually said to be 12–16 years, but cats, like humans, are living longer than they used to, and more and more are living into their 20s and even 30s. Also like humans, cats age at different rates, some remaining fit and active when advanced in years. Longevity depends on heredity as well as on standards of care.

Older cats need more warmth. In summer, they will spend hours sleeping in the sun; in winter, make sure they have a cozy bed.

Signs of age

Old cats gradually lose muscle tone, with spine, hip bones, and shoulders becoming more prominent and joints stiffening. Their fur often becomes thinner, and they feel the cold more. Hearing and sight may deteriorate, and they spend more time sleeping. There may also be changes in character: Some mellow, whereas others become cantankerous—just like humans.

Feline–Human Comparison

Cat's age	Human equivalent
Under 8 months	Childhood
8 months–2 years	Teenage years
1–2 years	Young adulthood
4–8 years	Middle age
8–13 years	Late middle age
13–17 years	Active retirement
17–19 years	Elderly
19–22 years	Ripe old age
Over 22 years	Centenarian

Care of the older cat

Old cats need consideration and a quiet environment without disturbances. A warm, soft bed in a quiet refuge should be provided. While respecting their need for more sleep, it is important to encourage moderate exercise with

Older cats spend much of their time sleeping, but they sleep more lightly, so a place where they can doze undisturbed is appreciated.

short, gentle play sessions. Stiffness and lack of energy may mean that some extra help with grooming is needed, including regular checks on claws, which may become overgrown.

Britain's oldest cat

Ma, a female tabby from Devon, died in 1957 aged 34 years 1 day, making her Britain's oldest reliably recorded cat. As a kitten, she almost died when she was caught in a gin trap. Because of this she was given extra care, which her owners believed was the secret of her long life. However, locals ascribed it to the powers of music, remembering that Ma spent hours listening to her owners playing Mozart and Beethoven.

World's oldest cat

Ma finally lost the title of oldest cat to Granpa, who died in 1998 aged 34 years 2 months. Granpa (officially Granpa Rexs Allen) was a pedigree Sphynx who had a checkered early life. Born in Paris and imported to the U.S., he escaped and spent time in a rescue shelter before achieving his final home. His longevity was ascribed to a happy life—which included a diet of bacon and eggs, broccoli, asparagus, and coffee.

Failing senses

Sight and hearing often deteriorate in older cats, but most cope well with disability, depending increasingly on their remaining senses, particularly smell, to compensate. Cats that are completely blind or deaf are safest kept indoors and allowed out only under close supervision to protect them from hazards they cannot sense.

Food and drink

Elderly digestive systems are less efficient, and cat foods made specifically for older cats are recommended. Old cats drink less, so a canned diet with a high water content helps to reduce the risk of dehydration and kidney problems. Loss of appetite may be caused by a failing sense of smell but could also be caused by dental ailments, so carry out regular checkups on teeth.

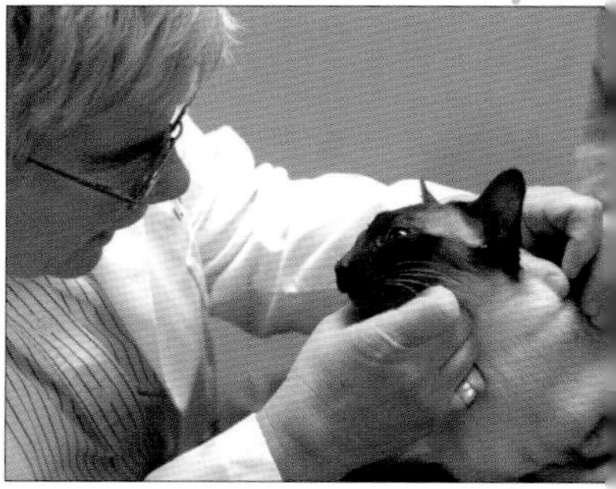

Regular dental checkups help to prevent feeding problems—and bad breath.

HOROSCOPES

Aries ***(March 21st–April 20th)***
Cats born under the sign of Aries are fun companions rather than restful pets—bold, energetic, and adventurous. Explorers and investigators, their curiosity can lead them into some tight corners, but they have a talent for survival. In a multicat household, the Aries cat tends to dominate other felines: he has to be first at the food dish and considers it his right to have an extra share of attention.

Taurus ***(April 21st–May 21st)***
The Taurean cat has a happy, easygoing personality and makes a cuddly pet. He likes his comforts, gravitating toward fireside seats and cozy beds, and regards his owner's lap as his home base. A regular routine gives him the security he appreciates, and he tends to be annoyed by disruptions to his approved schedule. He enjoys his food, and can become overweight if attention is not paid to his diet.

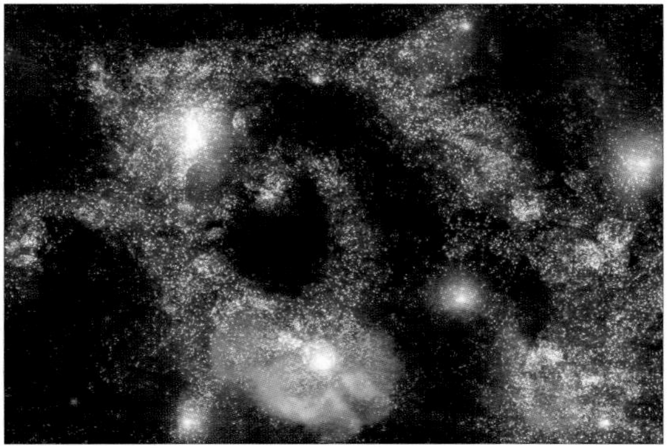

Is your cat's character written in the stars? Check his zodiac sign and make up your own mind.

Gemini ***(May 22nd–June 21st)***
Lively, fidgety, and often restless, the Gemini cat likes to be at the center of the action. He will flirt with your visitors, harass your local wildlife, and regard your furnishings as an adventure playground. He demands plenty of attention but offers it too. He is affectionate, and also the cat most likely to offer you a share of his dead mouse. Gemini cats stay kittens at heart well into old age.

Cancer ***(June 22nd–July 22nd)***
The Cancerian cat is a homebody and a lap cat that likes plenty of fuss—on his own terms. His highly sensitive nature means that he may seem shy or prickly at times, sporadically withdrawing from attention for reasons perfectly clear to himself but less so to his owners. However, he doesn't bear a grudge and will soon be his affectionate self again. Cancerian cats are often night owls.

Leo ***(July 23rd–August 22nd)***
The Leo cat is, in his own opinion at least, the king (or queen) of beasts. He expects to be the center of attention and treated with respect. So long as his human courtiers play their role and indulge all his little fads and quirks, however, he will repay them by being one of the most loving of companions. He is good-natured with other cats in the household so long as they accept that he is top cat.

Virgo ***(August 23rd–September 23rd)***
The Virgo cat likes to have things just so. A refined, even finicky cat who will not tolerate stale food left in bowls or a

A Celtic legend claims that cats' eyes are windows through which sensitive humans can gaze to see the world's mysteries unveiled.

dirty litter box, he likes a regular routine. He may be shy and withdrawn in a rowdy home, but is loving and responsive to owners who appreciate his needs. In a multicat household, he needs a private corner where he can withdraw from too much social life when he chooses.

Libra *(September 24th–October 23rd)*

The Libra cat is a sociable, outgoing creature who needs company and attention and doesn't thrive as a "home alone" cat. He enjoys making new acquaintances and will often appoint himself as household greeter of guests. Adaptable to most situations except neglect, he is a relaxed and relaxing presence in the home. Libra cats enjoy attention and respond particularly well to being groomed.

Scorpio *(October 24th–November 22nd)*

Scorpio cats can be demanding pets. Strong willed, highly focused, and active, they put everything they have into whatever they are doing at the moment, whether that be playing, demanding food, cuddling, or sleeping. The Scorpio cat is intensely affectionate to his owners, but can be a bully toward other felines in the household, or indeed in the neighborhood, as he is strongly territorial.

HOROSCOPES *(CONTINUED)*

Sagittarius *(November 23rd–December 21st)*

The Sagittarius cat is confident, energetic, and fond of his own way. He loves to explore and is happiest as an outdoor cat who can come and go as he pleases. He will delight his owner with hours of play, but may be slow to understand that claws and human skin don't go well together. Owners need to be considerate of his feelings, as he can be quick to take offense and slow to forgive a perceived insult.

Capricorn *(December 22nd–January 20th)*

Patience, persistence, and possessiveness are traits typical of the Capricorn cat. He likes his home comforts, and he likes routine, but he is not one to rush after things. Instead he is prepared to wait for what he wants, whether it be a favored chair or the fish on your plate. He is an affectionate creature who becomes very attached to his owners and makes a great family cat who is usually good with children and friendly with other household pets.

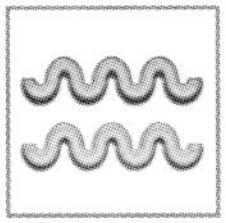

Aquarius *(January 21st–February 19th)*

The Aquarius cat is a one-of-a-kind individual, quirky, unpredictable, and full of personality and sometimes unpredictable. Intelligent, intuitive, and often highly inventive, he is an entertaining companion. He needs to be able to choose when to spend time with his family and when to take time out, but owners who respect his occasional need for privacy will find they have a friend for life.

Pisces *(February 20th–March 20th)*

The Pisces cat is a gentle, loving companion best suited to a peaceful home and a gentle owner. Pisces cats seem to sleep more than any other sign, perhaps because, like human Pisceans, they need time to dream. Highly sensitive to those they live with, they often seem to have extrasensory perception, coming just before they are called and knowing when their owners are coming home unexpectedly.

牛龙马羊兔蛇

The Year of the Cat			
Beginning	**Ending**	**Beginning**	**Ending**
February 2nd, 1927	January 22nd, 1928	February 11th, 1975	January 30th, 1976
February 19th, 1939	February 7th, 1940	January 29th, 1987	February 16th, 1988
February 6th, 1951	January 26th, 1952	February 16th, 1999	February 4th, 2000
January 25th, 1963	February 12th, 1964	February 15th, 2011	February 3rd, 2012

猪鼠狗虎猴鸡

Unlucky May kittens

In British folklore, kittens born in May were held to bring bad luck. A Welsh proverb says that, "Cats born in May bring snakes into the house," and English tradition says that May kittens grow up to be useless as mousers.

Blackberry kittens

British folklore also claims that Michaelmas Day (September 29th) is the date when Satan fell from Heaven to land in a blackberry bush—which is why you should not eat blackberries after Michaelmas, when the Devil spits on them, remembering the prickles. Kittens born after Michaelmas Day were tarred with the same brush. They were called "blackberry kittens" and said to be especially mischievous.

The cat did not feature in the original 12-year Chinese zodiac cycle because, legend has it, the rat failed to wake it up in time for the fateful meeting with Buddha. Today, however, the cat sometimes takes the place of the rabbit.

Eastern horoscopes

The Chinese zodiac runs through a cycle of 12 years, each having the sign of an animal: Rat, Ox, Tiger, Rabbit, Dragon, Snake, Horse, Sheep, Monkey, Rooster, Dog, and Pig. Legend says that when the gods were choosing animals for this honor, the rat tricked the cat out of having a place. However, in the Vietnamese zodiac the cat replaces the rabbit as the fourth animal, and today they are often considered interchangeable.

TRICKS AND TREATS

Why teach cats tricks?

People don't usually train cats. After all, the cat's independent character, which isn't geared to canine-style obedience, is part of his appeal for many cat owners. But teaching your cat to perform a few tricks is actually a handy way of building up your bond with him. From a cat's point of view, it means extra fuss and entertainment, provides valuable mental stimulation, and helps to improve his general confidence.

You can use a favorite catnip toy to gain a cat's attention when you start to train him.

Command/reward

The key idea is to teach your cat to associate a command with a reward. For example, if you want him to shake paws on request, touch his forepaw as you give the command "Shake." The touch will tempt him to move his paw. The moment he lifts it, give it a gentle shake and immediately give a food reward. Repeating this exercise a few times every day will teach your cat to offer his paw when asked.

Five Golden Rules for Cat Trainers

1. A lesson should be a treat for your cat, not a chore. Keep it fun!
2. Food rewards motivate cats—but keep tidbits tiny to prevent obesity.
3. Keep lessons short and regular, say, 10 minutes every day.
4. Schedule lessons before a meal to make food rewards more appealing.
5. Set lessons in a quiet environment with no distractions.

Food rewards

Start by identifying a treat that your cat will really want to work for. You need a healthful food item that can be served as tiny tidbits—you don't want to end up with a cat that is well educated but obese! Tuna flakes, scraps of hard cheese, or bits of cream cheese are often popular. Rewards must be immediate to be effective, so make sure you have the food at hand at the start of the lesson.

Clicker training

You can buy clickers (with instructions) in most pet shops. Teaching your pet to associate the clicker sound with a reward speeds up the learning process. Start by clicking the clicker and immediately offering a treat. Click, treat, and repeat until your cat knows that a click means a reward. Then introduce the clicker into lessons, clicking when the cat makes the right move to reinforce the desired behavior.

▲ *Little tidbits of food are ideal rewards in any training program. The* Sit *position can be encouraged by offering a tidbit above a cat or kitten's head, and moving it backward.*

Sit

Show your cat the reward, give the command *"Sit,"* and move the tidbit backward over his head. He is likely to sit to keep his balance as he leans back after the bait. If not, press gently down on his hindquarters to ease him into position. Never force him: If he is uncooperative, try again another day. As soon as he sits, praise or click and reward. Repeat a few times a day until he responds without a food bait.

Sit up and beg

Using the command "Up," hold the tidbit above your cat well out of his reach. When he sits up on his haunches and reaches for it, praise or click and give him the reward. (If he stands up on his hind legs instead of sitting up, move the food slowly over his head and he is likely to sit to keep his balance.) With regular repetition, he will learn to respond to the command without needing to see the food.

▼ *This kitten is a little overly enthusiastic, but he's on the right track. Skillful manipulation of the treat can make him sit back on his haunches in the desired* "Sit up and beg" *position.*

Wave

Starting when the cat is sitting down, give the command, *"Kitty, wave,"* and move the tidbit in front of him while keeping it just out of his reach. When she reaches out with a paw, praise or click and give him the reward. As she learns to associate the command with the paw movement, try to delay the reward until the movement more closely resembles a wave.

CATS BEHAVING BADLY (and how to cope)

Scratching furniture

You can **discourage** your pet from this behavior with a squirt from a water pistol or a sharp hand clap (cats hate sudden loud noises). You can **deter** him by protecting furniture with plastic film (cats dislike the feel). Most usefully, you can **distract** him from the furniture by providing a purpose-made scratching post to satisfy his need for claw maintenance, exercise, and scent marking.

Corners of furniture are quite vulnerable, and may need protection.

Toilet problems

Cats who soil in the house need a sympathetic approach. **Encourage** use of the litter box by providing a suitable location (well away from food bowls and with a degree of privacy) and perhaps try different litter types. **Discourage** use of other sites by cleaning soiled areas thoroughly to remove smell signals (avoid bleach, which gives the wrong message) and excluding your cat from such areas before their use becomes habitual.

Chewing houseplants

Protect plants (and your pet—many houseplants are poisonous to cats) by putting them out of reach if possible. You can **discourage** chewing with a squirt from a water pistol, and **deter** chewers by spraying leaves with diluted lemon juice or surrounding the plant with some kind of barrier. You can also **distract** your cat by providing him with his own pot of grass to nibble instead.

Biting

Cats who bite the hand that strokes them are usually individuals who are easily over-stimulated. **Avoid** putting them in this situation by restricting caresses to behind the ears, under the chin, or above the base of the tail: stroking down the back may be too much for them. Learn to **predict** the moment your cat has had enough—a tail twitch is the usual signal—and withdraw immediately.

If your cat bites fingers in play, stop allowing him access to your hands when playing and dangle toys from a safe distance instead.

Garden damage

If your cat digs up your flower beds and turns them into litter boxes, **deter** him by selective planting (lavender, rue, lemon thyme, or

Cats are great believers in self-service and may be tempted up onto kitchen counters by the presence of food, so make sure that any edibles are left securely covered.

anything prickly will put him off), by sprinkling commercial cat repellents or cayenne pepper, or by protecting bare soil with large stones. More expensive but very effective is a motion-activated sprinkler system. You can also **distract** your cat by planting an area especially for him with catnip.

Wool eating

Some cats become hooked on eating nonfood items, commonly wool or other fabrics, an addiction that endangers owners' clothes and cats' insides. This problem is hard to cure, but you may **deter** your cat with unpleasant-tasting sprays such as eucalyptus or menthol. You may also **distract** him by making his regular meals more challenging, providing tough chunks of meat that need concentrated chewing.

A cat who chews your possessions needs to be stopped for his own sake as well as yours. There is a real risk that he may swallow fragments that could lead to dangerous intestinal blockage.

Counter jumping

Cats like to observe the world from a high position, so it's natural for them to jump up onto kitchen work surfaces, dining tables, and the like. Quite apart from considerations of hygiene, this is an undesirable habit because of the dangers of hot food, sharp knives, and scalding stovetops. **Discourage** it with a stern "No!" and firm but gentle removal of the offender every time he jumps up, for his own safety.

Messy eaters

Cats can be very messy eaters, spreading food around the floor. **Encourage** them to use a plate by ensuring that bowls aren't tainted with the smell of old food or of detergent, and are wider than the maximum whisker span (cats hate getting their whiskers dirty). You can also **minimize** the problem by setting a wipe-clean mat under the bowl.

THE NAMING OF CATS

Three names...

As T. S. Eliot observes in his much-loved book of comic poetry, *Old Possum's Book of Practical Cats* (1939), "The Naming of Cats is a difficult matter." Eliot says that a cat must have three names: one for daily use ("such as Peter, Augustus, Alonso, or James"), one unique to himself and more distinguished ("such as Munkustrap, Quaxo, or Coricopat") and finally a "deep and inscrutable singular Name" known only to the cat himself. It certainly makes naming a tricky task!

...or two names

British folklore asserts that every cat should be given two names, one for use and one to be kept secret. The belief was that knowing a person's real name gave power over that person. Cats were all too prone to turn to the dark side, so it was safest not to let the Devil find out their names in the first place. So tradition recommends, "One for a secret, one for a riddle: name puss twice and befuddle the devil."

Reading the numbers

Want to understand your cat better? Try onomatomancy, a method of divination by names. Write down your cat's name, then beneath each letter put the number in which it occurs in the alphabet (1 for A, 2 for B, and so on). Add up the total, and if this comes into double figures, add those together to give a single figure. Check the meaning of that number on the chart below.

Adapting to circumstances

English philosopher Jeremy Bentham (1748–1832) had a cat called Sir John Langbourne, who was lively and somewhat mischievous. When the cat grew more sedate in middle age, Bentham changed his name to the Reverend John Langbourne—and in old age, when the cat had become "conspicuous for his gravity and philosophy" he became the Reverend Doctor John Langbourne.

Deliberately difficult

American author Samuel Longhorne Clemens, better known as Mark Twain, was a great cat lover. He chose unusual names for his pets,

Digit	Significance
1	An independent cat who likes to investigate the world
2	An amenable cat, sympathetic and adaptable to various lifestyles
3	A cat who enjoys life, sociable and eager to communicate
4	A calm cat who likes routine and order in his daily life
5	An adventurous cat who appreciates freedom to roam
6	A kind, serious cat, protective toward his family
7	A meditative cat who likes to think about things
8	A cat who wants to be boss in the household
9	A sweet-natured and gentle cat

Mark Twain poses with one of his many cats—but its name is unrecorded.

such as Apollinaris, Zoroaster, and Blatherskite, for the equally unusual reason that it would give his children practice in learning and pronouncing difficult words.

	Survey 1	Survey 2	Survey 3
1	Sooty	Charlie	Blackie
2	Tigger	Molly	Felix
3	Lucy	Snowy	Ginger
4	Smokey	Tigger	Kitty
5	Charlie	Poppy	Lucky
6	Smudge	Jasper	Sooty
7	Thomas	Millie	Tigger
8	Sam	Smudge	Tom
9	Misty	Lucy	Tabitha
10	Lucky	Blackie	Whiskers

Top ten

Surveys of the most popular cat names come up with varying results, perhaps because they can assess only small samples of a huge population. However, some names are common to all three of these recent "Top Ten" lists are shown in the chart at the top of this page.

What do you call an arty cat? Poussin! Lovers of puns can have great fun. What about Curl Hand Luke for a curly-coated Rex?

Naming a new breed

New breeds are named in many ways. The Ocicat was named for its looks—spotted like an Ocelot—and the Somali, a long-haired Abyssinian, for

The attractive Somali has nothing to do with Somalia, but was developed in the U.S. from long-haired Abyssinians.

Abyssinia's neighbor Somalia. The American Chantilly/Tiffany was first named after the Tiffany Theater in Los Angeles because it sounded classy, then renamed to avoid confusion with the British Tiffanie breed—and if that isn't confusing, what is?

INN SIGNS

A drink with the cat

Since 1393, when King Richard II ordered that all public houses and inns had to display a sign, British pub signs have displayed a wide variety of ingenious names. Cats feature in many of them, usually in combinations such as Cat and Fiddle, Cat and Bagpipes, Cat and Cabbage, or Cat and Canary, but sometimes solo as in Black Cat, Cheshire Cat, Fat Cat, Old Cat, and the occasional plain Cat.

Cat and Fiddle

Several pubs bear this name, which has a range of popular etymologies. It is often said to be a corruption of the name Caton le Fidèle ("the Faithful"), a medieval governor of Calais, France, or alternatively of Catherine le Fidèle, wife of Russian Czar Peter the Great. Some say it simply advertises games and music (tipcat being a popular sport)—or it may refer to the nursery rhyme "Hey diddle diddle, The cat and the fiddle."

Cats on inn signs may be Mad, Fat, Romping, or Rampant. There are Black Cats and Red Cats, a Cat With No Tail (on the Isle of Man, of course) and even a Burmese Cat—illustrated, confusingly, as a tiger.

Murder most foul

The Cat i' the Well (near Halifax, West Yorkshire) may be another name derived from a nursery rhyme ("Ding dong bell, Pussy's in the well"), but tradition claims a more sinister explanation. It is said that a former landlord murdered his wife, Cath, after discovering she was having an affair—and drowned her in the well.

Horrible heraldry

The Cat and Cabbage in Rotherham, Yorkshire, is said to derive its name from an adaptation of the badge of the York & Lancaster Regiment, which depicts a tiger and a rose. Another mangled heraldic sign is that of the Charlton Cat in Charlton St. Peter, Wiltshire, formerly the Poores Arms with a coat of lion including a lion, which locals nicknamed a "cat."

Blame the sign painter!

Locals, bemused by the painting of a griffin on the inn sign, nicknamed the Downing Arms (Tadlow, Huntingdonshire) the Scratching Cat. The Downing Arms is now closed, but the

Feline pub names include corruptions such as the Cat and Wheel (once the Catherine Wheel) and puzzles such as the Cat and Custard Pot. Others originate from literature or local lore.

former White Lion at Pidley, Cambridgeshire, remains open under a new name that reflects customers' opinions of the badly painted lion on the sign—the Mad Cat.

Scottish raiders

Pubs called the Cat and Bagpipes occur across northern Britain. The name may come from folk songs like the Cat and Fiddle tradition, but is said to be a corruption of "cateran" (a Highland irregular soldier), a reminder of the days when the skirl of bagpipes announced the coming of Scottish border raiders to plunder English homesteads.

Salutation and Cat

London's Salutation and Cat achieved fame as the lodgings of 18th-century poet Samuel Taylor Coleridge, who lived there until 1795 when he was ejected for being unable to pay his bill. Its name is an extraordinary combination of religious icon (the salutation of Angel Gabriel to the Virgin Mary) and popular sport, the "cat" signifying that the game of tipcat was played inside.

Local features

The Squinting Cat at Harrogate, Yorkshire, is said to be named for a former lady, known as "t'owd cat" from her habit of squinting through the curtains to scrutinize approaching customers. But the Red Cat Hotel (near King's Lynn, Norfolk) is named for a real, though deceased, feline—a mummified cat found in the walls and now proudly displayed in a glass case.

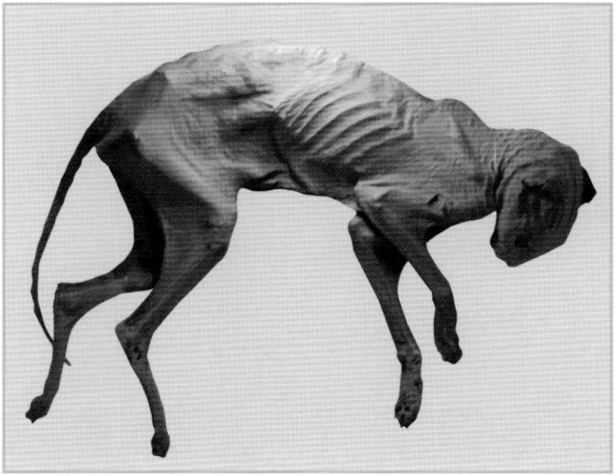

The mummified cat of the Red Cat Hotel was found in a roof space by the present owner's grandfather and is on display in an illuminated case in the main bar.

PEOPLE, PLACES, AND BEASTS

Pussy Galore

In Ian Fleming's seventh James Bond novel, *Goldfinger,* the statutory "Bond girl," to be immortalized in the 1964 movie by Honor Blackman, has the unusual name of Pussy Galore. She was named after one of Fleming's pets—not a cat, but an octopus! The author's fascination with this species later led to another title, *Octopussy.*

Cat mountains?

New York State's Catskill Mountains are said to owe their name (Dutch "cat creek") to a local prevalence of bobcats. However, other theories abound, deriving the name from Dutch *kat*, "tennis racquet" (referring to the game of lacrosse played by Iroquois natives), Dutch *kasteel* "fortification" (referring to Native American stockades), a ship named *The Cat,* and even a Dutch poet, Jacob Cats.

The Catskill Mountains boast the highest waterfall in New York State, Katterskill Falls.

Jane Fonda as Cat Ballou, an outlaw intent upon avenging her father's death.

Kitty Hawk

The plane in which the Wright brothers achieved the world's first powered aircraft flight in 1903 is often miscalled the *Kitty Hawk*, but its creators knew it simply as *The Flyer*. Its flight took place at Kitty Hawk, North Carolina, whose name probably comes from the native "Chickahauk," meaning "goose hunting grounds." An alternative theory derives it from "skeeter hawk," the local name for the area's abundant dragonflies.

Western heroine

Cat Ballou, a 1965 comedy Western film, tells the story of a woman who hires a famous gunman to avenge her father's murder, but finds him to be a drunken has-been. Heroine Cat Ballou is played by Jane Fonda. Her feline name is an abbreviation: shortening her given name of Catherine to Cat reflects the development from prim schoolteacher Miss Catherine to resolute outlaw, Cat.

Kuching boasts many cat statues as well as a Cat Museum, in honor of its "cat" name.

Cat city?

The capital city of Sarawak, East Malaysia, is Kuching—a name that means "cat." Legend says that when Englishman Sir James Brooke became ruler of Sarawak in 1841, he pointed to this city and asked his guide its name. Thinking he was pointing at a feral cat scavenging at the riverside, the guide answered in his own language, "Cat" thus accidentally renaming the city.

Wild cousins

"Cat" place-names in Britain generally refer to the European wildcat, once found across the country but now restricted to Scotland. Examples include Cat Bells ("wildcats' den") and Cattrig Force ("wildcats' ridge waterfall"), both in the Lake District, and Cassop ("wildcats' valley") in County Durham. In the U.S., most "cat" place-names, like the many Cat Mountains, refer to cougars, lynx, or bobcats.

Mislabeled

Several vaguely catlike species bear the name of "cat" without having any right to it. Australia has its marsupial Native Cat. Britain has its Polecat, a relative of the ferret, and its cousin the Pine Marten is also known as the Marten-Cat and Tree Cat. Africa's Civet is often called the Civet-Cat, and the same name is frequently misapplied to America's Cacomistle, a raccoon relative also known as the Ringtail Cat and Miner's Cat.

Cat Stevens

When Stephen Demetre Georgiou broke into the pop music business in the 1960s, his first move was to pick a catchier name, and it was as Cat Stevens that he became a popular singer and songwriter. Reportedly he picked the name Cat because of a girl who told him he had eyes like a cat. A little inappropriately, his first hit song was *I Love My Dog*. In 1978, as a convert to Islam, he changed his name to Yusuf Islam.

Cat Stevens was a well-known name in the 1960s and 1970s, registering sales in excess of 40 million albums in that period.

KIT AND KABOODLE

The cherry-colored cat

Showman Phineas Barnum, a great exploiter of public curiosity, drew crowds when he announced that he was exhibiting the world's first cherry-colored cat. The people who flocked to see it were baffled and angry to find an ordinary black cat on display—but when they demanded their money back, Barnum pointed out cheerfully, and correctly, that some cherries are indeed black.

Showman Phineas Barnum, photographed in 1862 with one of his famous attractions, the midget Commodore George Washington Nutt.

First handbook

The first serious book on cats was written by François-Augustin Paradis de Moncrif (1687–1770). *Histoire des Chats*, published in 1727, was written as a defense of a much abused species, but Moncrif's belief that "one day we shall see the merit of Cats generally recognized" was too far ahead of its time. His book met with such ridicule that a few years later he felt forced to withdraw it from circulation. How he must be laughing now!

Blood donors

Animal hospitals use feline blood donors to provide transfusions for injured cats, but, just as with humans, they need to check blood type.

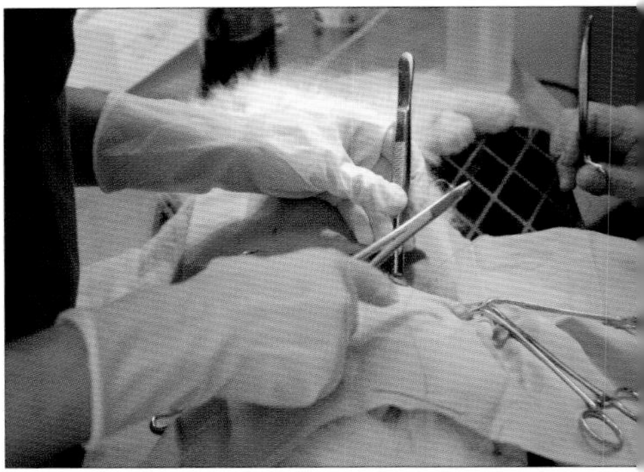

Feline blood donors save the lives of other cats, at no cost to themselves. They are well tended, for only healthy cats are suitable.

Cats have three blood types—A (commonest), B, and AB (rarest)—and there is no "universal donor" feline blood type, so using the wrong one can kill. Cats need blood transfusions more rarely than dogs, but some vets keep resident donors on hand for emergencies.

A cat's revenge

A she-cat called Pudlenka arrived on the doorstep of Czech playwright Karel Capek (1890–1938) the very day that his Angora tomcat was poisoned, and immediately set about filling the house with kittens. As she produced litter after litter (and was joined in the task by daughters and granddaughters) Capek concluded that her task was to "revenge and replace a hundredfold the life of that tomcat."

Familiars forgiven

In the 16th and 17th centuries, the town of Prestonpans was one of Scotland's witch-hunting centers: 81 supposed witches were condemned and executed at the local court, often on grounds as slight as ownership of a black cat. At Halloween 2004 the court celebrated its last session before closing down by announcing official pardons for the witch hunt's victims—and, readers will surely be glad to note, "all the cats concerned."

Schrödinger's cat

The "Schrödinger's cat" paradox was outlined by Austrian physicist Erwin Schrödinger (1887–1961) to illustrate the idea of "'superposition" in quantum mechanics theory. The principle of superposition supposes that although we do not know what the state of any object is, it is actually in all possible states simultaneously, as long as we don't look to check. Schrödinger's analogy proposes a sealed box containing a live cat and a canister of poison gas that has a 50 percent chance of being triggered. Until the box is opened, the cat's chances of being alive or dead are equal—so until that time, according to quantum law it may be considered both.

Erwin Schrödinger's postulated his famous "cat paradox" as a metaphor to illustrate quantum law, not as a practical experiment!

Loopy laws

Several American states and cities have distinctly unusual laws limiting a cat's legal activities. Louisiana has a law prohibiting cats from chasing ducks in city streets, Dallas requires cats to wear headlights when walking the streets after dark, and Idaho strictly forbids them to intercede in a dog fight. In Natchez, Mississippi, cats are not legally permitted to drink beer, even if they are of age.

Kellas cats

Reports of mysterious "black panthers" across Britain were given a boost in the early 1980s, when Scottish gamekeepers caught a number of very large black cats. These "Kellas cats" (named for a Morayshire village) were thought at first to be a new species, but are now known to be hybrids between Scottish wildcats and domestic ferals. Rumors of a strain of giant "King Kellas" cats roaming the glens of Scotland remain unproved.

DOGS, HORSES, AND OTHER FRIENDS

Key Rules for Cat-Dog Introductions	
1 Remember rewards	Help things along by encouraging both animals to associate meeting each other with favorite tidbits. Rewards for being friendly work much better than punishment for misbehavior.
2 No chasing	Don't give the dog a chance to chase the cat. Supervise early meetings and use a crate or leash to prevent the dog from finding out that cat chasing is fun.
3 Beware of the claws	A cat's claws can blind a dog. Watch out for signs that the cat is scared or angry, and also supervise play—kittens may be slow to learn claw control.

Cats and dogs

The main reason why cats and dogs are traditionally considered enemies is the combination of the dog's inborn chasing instinct and the cat's natural flight instinct. Few dogs can resist chasing a fleeing cat! More aggressive cats will swipe a dog's nose instead of running away, which doesn't help the situation. However, cats and dogs that live together are often the best of friends.

Cats' best friend

Between 1990 and 2005 an American dog called Ginny became famous as "the dog who loved cats." Starting by rescuing a litter of kittens trapped in a pipe, she went on to save more than 900 endangered felines, even digging through broken glass to find an injured cat. In 1998 her dedication earned her the title of "Cat [sic] of the Year," and her memorial service in 2005 was attended by 300 cats.

Cat and squirrel

When wildlife photographer John Paling set out to film a study of the gray squirrel, he had a batch of baby squirrels to raise by hand. This proved a difficult task, until a tortie-and-white cat called Beauty came to the rescue. Despite falling ill with cat flu while feeding her kittens and Sammy the squirrel, she proved a devoted mother and raised Sammy to become the star of the film.

Sugar was another feline mother who happily adopted a baby squirrel among her kittens.

Godolphin Arabian

The Godolphin Arabian, one of the three great 18th-century stallions who formed the foundation of modern racing thoroughbreds, was inseparable from his stable companion, a black cat called Grimalkin. The bond between horse and cat was so strong that when the Godolphin Arabian died, his feline friend remained with his body until its burial and died shortly afterward, reportedly of a broken heart.

Grimalkin appears in several portraits of the Godolphin Arabian. George Stubbs turned him into a tabby so he would show up better.

Cat and rat

Cases of cats adopting babies of other species are not uncommon, so when naturalist Frances Pitt (1888–1964) offered a baby rat to Granny, her tabby-and-white cat, she was not surprised that he was accepted. However, Granny was even more careful with the little rat than with her own kittens. Named Samuel Whiskers, he grew up to be a great pet, and he and Granny were devoted friends throughout his life.

THE NEW AGE CAT

Massage

When stroking becomes massage, it can be highly beneficial. Using small circular motions of thumb and fingertips, start on each side of the spine and work along the cat's back, shoulders, sides, and hind legs, then move on to the chest, belly, and finally forelegs. Pay attention to your cat's response: Many cats regard their bellies as a no-go area, and the back of the hind legs is sometimes also a sensitive area.

Massage is not only beneficial to a cat's health, but an opportunity for bonding with its owner.

T-touch massage

This is a form of massage developed for treating horses and domestic pets by animal behaviorist Linda Tellington-Jones, in which various patterns of small circular finger movements are worked around the body. Designed to relax and reassure the patient, it is employed to resolve stress, to ease sprains, strains, and other muscle or bone disorders, and to create a bond between pet and owner.

Alternative therapies

The "alternative" label covers a broad spectrum of treatments, some recognized and often employed by vets as valuable complements or indeed alternatives to conventional methods, others distinctly dubious. All such treatments should be used only with the guidance of qualified experts, to avoid inappropriate use that may be useless or even dangerous to your pet.

Aromatherapy

Aromatherapy oils can assist with ailments from respiratory problems to digestive upsets. However, unlike humans and dogs, cats can be made seriously or even fatally ill if these oils are given orally or even massaged into the skin. Instead, heat the oil in a diffuser for the cat to inhale, and shut him in a room with it twice daily for five days. Consult a trained aromatherapist to select appropriate oils.

Take care, if using a candle-heated oil diffuser, to site it where the cat cannot come into contact with the flame.

Acupuncture isn't a "quick fix"—a course of treatment usually entails six to eight visits—but at least it has no adverse side effects.

Acupuncture

Acupuncture, the painless insertion of small needles at specific points on the body to stimulate self-healing, has been adopted by a growing number of vets who believe it helps in the treatment of pain, chronic digestive disturbances, epilepsy, and other ailments. There is strong anecdotal evidence of its effectiveness, particularly as pain relief.

Homeopathy

Homeopathic remedies consist of "treating like with like" via intensely diluted doses of substances that would, at full strength, cause the symptoms that are to be treated, and that are said to trigger the body's immune system. There is heated debate as to whether homeopathy is valuable or useless, but many users report a good success rate. Take advice before using, and follow instructions closely.

Magnet therapy

This treatment is based on treating ailments by exposure to magnetic fields. Specialized magnets worn on the body (in the case of cats, on a collar) are said to relieve pain and speed healing. This is another technique on which the jury is still out, but many people have reported that cats (particularly elderly arthritic animals) improved in health when provided with magnetic collars.

Herbal medicine

Proprietary herbal remedies made specifically for cats can provide safe and effective treatment, or infusions of fresh herbs can be made at home. Always obtain expert guidance before using herbal medicines, as in some cases overdosage can be fatal. It is best to obtain a vet's diagnosis in the first place, as treating a sick cat on a trial basis is tantamount to neglect, or even cruelty.

- *Don't try to mix your own herbal medicines without training—always seek expert advice.*

CATTY DICTIONARY

Catbird – This American songbird, related to the thrush, earned its name from its song, which includes catlike mewing notes.

Cat burglar – One who breaks into houses and makes his entry with the stealth of a cat stalking its prey.

Catfish – This fish is named for the long barbels near its mouth, which resemble a cat's whiskers but are actually fleshy sensory organs used to detect food.

Catgut – A strong thread formerly used for violin strings and made from sheep's intestines – not those of cats! The name may derive from a fancied resemblance of the sound of violins to caterwauling. It is also said that early makers of sheep-gut strings claimed to use cats' intestines to discourage competitors, since it was held to be bad luck to kill a cat.

Cathouse – This slang term for a brothel dates back to the 15th century when prostitutes were colloquially called "cats" in an apparent reference to feline promiscuity.

Catkins – The dangling flowers of willows, birches, hazels, etc. are called catkins from their resemblance to tiny cats' tails.

Cat-o'-nine-tails – A whip with nine cord lashes, possibly named because it left welts such as cat scratches, and formerly used to flog offenders in the British army and navy. A brutal practice, flogging was abhorred by leaders such as Admiral Nelson, but harsh officers often sentenced men to receive hundreds of lashes with the cat.

Cat's claw – A rain-forest vine found in South America and Asia that climbs to a height of up to 100 ft. (30 m) by means of small curved thorns ('claws') at the base of the leaves, with which it attaches itself to nearby trees. The bark and roots are used in herbal medicine to combat inflammation and boost the immune system.

Cat's cradle – A game in which a string is looped on the fingers to form an intricate pattern between the player's hands. Two players can pass the "cradle" back and forth to form more complicated designs. Found all over the world, this ancient game may once have been a religious ritual connected with worship of the sun god.

Cat's-eye – A semiprecious stone that displays a narrow band of reflected light, resembling the luster of a cat's eyes. Several different minerals are given this name, including quartz and chrysoberyl.

Cat's-paw – A ripple on the surface of the sea caused by a light breeze, touching the water as delicately as a cat's paw.

Cat's-tail – Several species of plants with long fluffy "tail-like" seed heads, including various sedges and rushes, are commonly called cat's-tails.

Catwalk – A narrow raised walkway, such as that set above theater stages for technicians or the platform used by fashion models. The term derives from cats' ability to walk confidently along high narrow routes such as the tops of fences.

CATTY COMMENTS

Everyday expressions often feature cats. Some are self-explanatory, like **"tomcatting around"** or **"looking like something the cat brought in." "Catty remarks"** sting like a cat's claws, and a **"scaredy-cat"** has a cat's wariness. **"Curiosity killed the cat"** refers to the cat's tendency to get into trouble investigating hazards—and **"cats have nine lives"** reflects their ability to get out of it. Other expressions need some explanation.

To let the cat out of the bag *(To give away a secret.)* Piglets were transported to market in sacks, and a con man might try to cheat buyers by offering a wriggling bag with a worthless cat inside. Opening the bag to check it gave the game away by letting the cat out of the bag.

No room to swing a cat *(With very little space.)* In the days of naval floggings, the entire ship's company was called on deck to witness punishment. If the deck was crowded, the bosun could not use his cat-o'-nine-tails without hitting bystanders—he had no room to swing his cat.

To fight like Kilkenny cats *(To fight furiously.)* Legend says that German soldiers stationed in Kilkenny, Ireland, amused themselves by hanging two cats up together by their tails to set them fighting. When an officer approached, they hastily severed the tails to release the cats, explaining away the evidence with the claim that two cats had fought so savagely that only their tails were left.

See which way the cat jumps *(See which way a situation develops before acting.)* This is another expression from the bad old days of cruel sports. In this case, the cat was placed up a tree as a target and the marksmen had to wait to see which way the cat jumped before pulling the trigger.

To put the cat among the pigeons *(To cause alarm by revealing a controversial fact.)* Anyone who has seen the enormous flap when a flock of pigeons is suddenly startled by a cat will understand this one; but it is said to have been inspired by yet another bloodsport. When the British governed India, a popular amusement was to put a wildcat in a pigeon pen and bet on how many birds the cat could swat with one swipe of its paw.

Sitting in the catbird seat *(Being in an advantageous position.)* Catbirds tend to choose the highest available perch from which to sing, above everyone else. The phrase first appeared in print in 1942 in James Thurber's humorous short story *The Catbird Seat* after being popularized by famous radio baseball commentator "Red" Barber, who said that he picked it up in Cincinnati in the 1930s.

Like a cat on hot bricks/a hot tin roof *(Nervous, uneasy, and fidgety.)* Cats love a warm seat, and are reluctant to move even when it becomes too warm for comfort. Tennessee Williams's play *Cat on a Hot Tin Roof* (1955) popularized the phrase, although in the U.K., where tin roofs are less common, "a cat on hot bricks" is more common.

To play cat and mouse with someone *(To torment someone who is in your power.)* A cat playing with a mouse pretends to release it, then pounces again.

INDEX

Page numbers set in *italics* refer to picture captions.

Photographic Credits

The Algonquin Hotel, New York: 88 top right.
The Art Archive: 12 left (Musée du Louvre, Paris/Dagli Orti), 14 left (Harper Collins Publishers), 14 right (Genius of China Exhibition), 81 bottom right (Culver Pictures), 92 top (Jarrold Publishing), 96 left (British Museum/Dagli Orti [A]), 114 bottom (Galleria Borghese, Rome/Dagli Orti [A]), 138 center left (Museo del Prado, Madrid/Dagli Orti), 139 center right (Tate Gallery, London/Eileen Tweedy), 146 right (Private Collection/Marc Charmet), 148 center (Culver Pictures), 149 center left (Culver Pictures), 165 top (Michael O'Mara Books), 192 top left.
Elizabeth Bradley Ltd: 165 bottom left.
The Bridgeman Art Library: 115 top (Nationalmuseum, Stockholm), 144 center right (Boughton House, Northamptonshire), 163 bottom left (Private Collection/Bonham's, London).
Jane Burton, Warren Photographic: 2, 11, 27 bottom left, 28 bottom left, 41 bottom, 42-3, 43 right, 49 top right, 52 bottom, 60 top right, 62 bottom left, 62-3, 70 top, 74 top, 75 top, 76 bottom, 79, 111, 115 bottom right, 133 top, 143, 182, 183 top left, 183 center right, 196 left (cat).
City of Coventry Armorial Bearings: 113 top.
William J. Clinton Presidential Library: 106 bottom.
Cristal Lalique: 163 top.
***The Daily News*, Taranaki Newspapers, New Zealand:** 89 bottom left (Mark Dwyer), 97 bottom left.
Sam Douglas: 132 bottom center.
Chris Elliott: 83 bottom left.
Dr Sharon Ellman-Murray: 98 top right.
EMPICS: 87 bottom right (AP Photo/Christophe Ena).
Holly Erickson, www.enchanted-tails.com: 162 top.
The Famous Grouse Distillery: 70 bottom center and right.
Alan Fleming: 109 bottom right.
Fortean Picture Library: 125 center left (Philip Carr), 154 center left.
Green Piece Wire Art: 170, 171 (with thanks to Brad Granatier).
Rowan Guthrie, Port Taranaki, New Zealand: 83 center right.
The Inn Sign Society: 188 top right.
In-Press Photography Ltd: 103 bottom right.
Interpet Archive: 64 top, 64 center left, 65 top, 69 bottom right, 72 top, 75 bottom, 76 top, 150 both, 151 top left, 151 bottom, 152 center left, 152 top right, 156 bottom left, 157 top, 174 center left, 174 bottom right.
iStockphoto.com/
AtWaG: 161.
Ira Bachinskaya: 179 top, 187 right.
Anne Gro Bergesen: 17 top, 25 bottom right, 27 bottom right, 29 center right, 51 top right, 105 center right.
Verna Bice: 65 bottom left.
Matt Billings: 125 top right.
Brandon Blinkenberg: 46 top.
Eric Louie Bolante: 53 bottom right.
Braddy: 73 bottom left.
Alex Bramwell: 4, 5, 89 top right, 153 top.
Dan Brandenburg: 107 inset coin.
Alexander Briel: 165 bottom right.
Alon Brik: 37 top right, 141 top left.
Daniel Brunner: 196 center left.
Peter Chen: 178-180 (symbols).
Joey Chung: 52 top.
Odelia Cohen: 48 top.
Christiane Cornelius: 1 (zodiac), 180 (zodiac).
Andrew Dean: 53 top.
Andrew de Bezenac: 86 center left.
Julie de Leseleuc: 77 top right, 181 (Chinese characters).
Edzard de Ranitz: 57 bottom.
Roel Dillen: 156 center.
Sharon Dominick: 22 top, 57 top left, 157 bottom right, 185 bottom.
Kristen Eckstein: 94 bottom.
David Edwards: 149 top.
Firehorse: 50 left.
Ron Fothergill: 184 center right.
Dirk Freder: 164 bottom left.
Lise Gagne: 158 bottom left.
Jose Gil: 35 top.
Johanna Goodyear: 131 bottom center.
Matthew Gough: 164 top right.
Naomi Hasegawa: 66 left.
Mark Hayes: 145 right.
Justin Horrocks: 46 bottom.
Dave Huss: 107 top right.
Melanie Jensen: 49 top left.
Jeremy Johnson: 95 bottom.
Sandy Jones: 177 top left.
Ewelina Kadyla: 68 center left.
Sergey Kashkin: 131 bottom right.
Maxim Kazitov: 118 bottom left.
Khr128: 176 center left.
Jason Koenig: 55 bottom right.
Arthur Kwiatkowski: 177 bottom left.
Jim Larkin: 179 (inset).

Ivonne Lehner: 58 left.
Leeuwtje: 195 top left.
Candice Lo: 156 top right.
Sue Loader: 108 left.
Valerie Loiseleux: 127 top left.
Tina Lorien: 160 bottom right.
Nancy Louie: 105 top left, 151 center right, 177 bottom right.
Dianne Maire: 55 top left.
Jon McIntosh: 77 bottom left.
Denise McQuillen: 56 center left.
Martina Misar: 20.
Krzysztof Nieciecki: 117 center left.
Ingrid Oliphant: 108 top right.
Remigiusz Oprzadek: 176 top.
Alon Othnay: 192 top right.
Brian Palmer: 190 center left.
Lee Pettet: 163 bottom right.
Fielding Piepereit: 1 (cat), 180 (cat), 184 top right.
Kate Place: 73 top right.
Jillian Pond: 60 bottom left.
Oleg Prikhodko: 54 bottom right.
Robh: 102.
Ronen: 144 top left.
Ben Scholz: 104 bottom.
Matthew Scherf: 159 center left (inset of tin).
Sherry Schuller: 136 top.
Bonnie Schupp: 33 right.
Natalia Semenchuk: 48 left.
SharAmbrosia: 160 center left, 197 bottom right.
Suzannah Skelton: 60 top left.
Carolina K. Smith, MD: 140 bottom right.
Holly Smith: 109 left.
Chuck Spidell: 63 bottom.
Vladimir Suponev: 44 bottom, 58 top right.
Rob Sylvan: 120 top.
Melanie Taylor: 134 bottom.
Andrei Tchernov: 174 top right.
Christy Thompson: 54 center left.
Marek Tihelka: 72 bottom left.
Govinda Trazo: 116 top.
Maartje van Caspel: 42 top.
Vasiliki Varvaki: 64 bottom right, 68 top right.
Vasil Vasilev: 30 left.
Fer Vernik: 93 bottom.
Angelo Villaschi: 44 left.
Alex Vlassov: 47.
Tanya Weliky: 56 bottom left, 117 bottom right.
Janine White: 39 bottom, 112 left.
Monika Wisniewska: 8, 185 top.
Gisele Wright: 196 bottom right.
Sherry Yates: 122 top, 152 bottom.
Rafal Zdeb: 6, 103 top.
The Kobal Collection: 87 center left (©Walt Disney), 124 (Toho), 134 top (Paramount), 135 bottom right (ABC/Viacom), 190 top right (Columbia).
Mary Evans Picture Library: 80 center left, 84 bottom left, 97 center right, 104 top, 106 center left, 154 center right (Maurice Ambler), 158 top, 187 top left, 193 bottom left.
Moscow Cats Theatre: 96 center left.
Shirley Rousseau Murphy: 133 center right.
PDSA: 82 (all three), 93 top.
Pictorial Press Ltd: 136 bottom left (©Warner Bros).
De Poezenboot: 155 both bottom.
Popperfoto: 147 top.
Purina Hall of Fame: 100 bottom left, 101.
Red Cat Hotel, North Wootton: 189 bottom.
Rex Features: 18 top, 22 bottom (Derek Ironside), 23 top (Askov Press), 30 bottom (Images), 38 left (Nils Jorgensen), 57 center right (Lewis Whyld), 67 top left (Photoreporters Inc.), 69 center left (Action Press), 85 top (Nils Jorgensen), 85 bottom (Assignments), 90 center right (Jonathan Hordle), 94 top, 95 top (Michael Norcia), 99 (Sipa Press), 130 top (©Universal/Everett), 135 top (©Columbia/Everett), 137 top (© Hanna-Barbera/Everett), 146 left (Everett Collection), 155 top (Jonathan Hordle), 195 center right (Nils Jorgensen), 197 top left (Sinopix).
Patrick Roberts, www.purr-n-fur.org.uk: 43 center, 84 top, 162 left group, 189 top row.
Sarawak Tourism Board: 191 top left.
The Savoy Hotel, London: 121 bottom.
Shakespeare's Globe Theatre, London: 90 left.
Topfoto: 12 right (The British Museum), 13 left (Charles Walker), 40 left and inset (LNB), 67 center right (Bandphoto/Uppa.co.uk), 81 top left, 98 bottom left (Fortean), 116 bottom right (Fortean), 118 top (Collection Roger-Viollet), 119 right (Charles Walker), 120 center left, 126 top left (Charles Walker), 126 top right (Topham Picturepoint), 127 bottom right (Charles Walker), 128 center left (Topham Picturepoint), 129 left (Novosti), 129 right, 137 bottom right (FP), 138 top right (The British Museum/HIP), 139 bottom left (Collection Roger-Viollet), 140 top left (The British Museum/HIP), 141 bottom right, 191 bottom right (UPPA Ltd).
The Lewis Walpole Library, Yale University: 31 top.
The White House: 107 center left (Paul Morse).
www.donmarquis.org: 128 top.